The Voice of Vatican II

Words for Our Church Today

PETER A. HUFF, PHD

Liguori
ONE LIGUORI DRIVE
LIGUORI MO 63057-9999

Imprimi Potest:
Harry Grile, CSsR, Provincial, Denver Province, The Redemptorists

Published by Liguori Publications, Liguori, Missouri 63057

To order, call 800-325-9521, or visit liguori.org

Library of Congress Cataloging-in-Publication Data

Huff, Peter A.
The voice of Vatican II : words for our church today / Peter A. Huff.
p. cm.
Includes bibliographical references (p.79).
ISBN 978-0-7648-1984-1
1. Catholic Church—Doctrines. 2. Vatican Council (2nd : 1962-1965) I. Title.
BX1751.3.H84 2012
230'.2—dc23
2012011430

Printed in the United States of America
16 15 14 13 12 / 5 4 3 2 1
First Edition

Contents

Preface

Several years ago, I was a Baptist chaplain serving in a Catholic hospital. I had long been intrigued with the Roman Catholic tradition and wanted to get better acquainted with it. The hospital's priest suggested I read the documents of Vatican II. I followed his advice and have been reading them ever since. In fact, I read them all the way into the Catholic Church.

My encounter with the documents of the Second Vatican Council was a life-changing experience. Yours can be, too, whether you are a newcomer to the Church or a lifelong practitioner of the faith. This book is designed for the first-time reader of the council's documents. It introduces you to the message of Vatican II and explains why that message is so important for us today. In the council's teachings, you will discover an inspiring vision of Christian discipleship for the present age.

Many people have shaped my evolving understanding of Vatican II and contributed to the development of this book and its companion volume, *Vatican II: Its Impact on You*. I especially want to thank Professor Ronald Modras, who first introduced me to the theology of the council; Father Mathew J. Kessler, CSsR, who ardently supported this project from the beginning; and my wife, Mary, whose keen editorial eye and sense of style have always made me a better writer. I alone am responsible for any errors of fact or interpretation.

Unless otherwise noted, Scripture quotations are taken from the *New Revised Standard Version of the Bible*. Quotations from Vatican II documents come from an edition of the texts prepared by Father Austin Flannery; each reference includes the document's Latin title or its abbreviation and the number of the relevant paragraph or section. Other Church documents cited in the book can be found on the Works Cited page or the Vatican website (www.vatican.va).

Abbreviations of Vatican II Documents

(AA)   *Apostolicam Actuositatem*: Decree on the Apostolate of the Laity

(AG)   *Ad Gentes*: Decree on the Church's Missionary Activity

(CD)   *Christus Dominus*: Decree on the Bishops' Pastoral Office in the Church

(DH)   *Dignitatis Humanae*: Declaration on Religious Freedom

(DV)   *Dei Verbum*: Dogmatic Constitution on Divine Revelation

(GE)   *Gravissimum Educationis*: Declaration on Christian Education

(GS)   *Gaudium et Spes*: Pastoral Constitution on the Church in the Modern World

(IM)   *Inter Mirifica*: Decree on the Instruments of Social Communication

(LG)   *Lumen Gentium*: Dogmatic Constitution on the Church

(NA)   *Nostra Aetate*: Declaration on the Relationship of the Church to Non-Christian Religions

(OE)   *Orientalium Ecclesiarum*: Decree on Eastern Catholic Churches

(OT)   *Optatam Totius*: Decree on Priestly Formation

(PC)   *Perfectae Caritatis*: Decree on the Appropriate Renewal of the Religious Life

(PO)   *Presbyterorum Ordinis*: Decree on the Ministry and Life of Priests

(SC)   *Sacrosanctum Concilium*: Constitution on the Sacred Liturgy

(UR)   *Unitatis Redintegratio*: Decree on Ecumenism

Introduction

The Second Vatican Council (1962-1965) was one of the greatest events of the twentieth century. Men and women from all over the world participated in its sessions and the implementation of its decisions. Many others, from a wide variety of cultures and creeds, followed its developments through the international media. Vatican II was the first Church council ever to be covered by radio and television.

In the end, though, Vatican II was about ideas, some conventional, some controversial, all critically important. We find these ideas, of course, expressed in words—thousands and thousands of words. On paper they consume anywhere from 500 to 700 pages in a standard collection of the council texts. Today the many words of Vatican II also exist in cyberspace. The Latin originals and English versions are widely available. The Vatican website provides translations in several different languages, including Chinese and Swahili. We often speak of the spirit of Vatican II. The only way truly to know the substance of its message, however, is through direct encounter with the words of its documents.

Sixteen documents were written, debated, and approved by the Second Vatican Council. These texts are now part of the Church's ever-expanding body of official or magisterial teaching (from the Latin for "master" or "authority"). The documents are quoted in the *Catechism of the Catholic Church*, nearly every papal letter and speech, countless theological and devotional publications, and any number of Sunday homilies. They reverberate daily in our prayers and our private meditations. Some passages, thanks to the force of their beauty and wisdom, rival the best of the Christian literary heritage. These records are the voice of Vatican II, the voice of the Church today.

Vatican II's Sixteen Documents

The sixteen documents are divided into three categories, and each has an official Latin title.

Four documents are constitutions:

- Constitution on the Sacred Liturgy (*Sacrosanctum Concilium*),
- Dogmatic Constitution on the Church (*Lumen Gentium*, also called *De Ecclesia*),
- Dogmatic Constitution on Divine Revelation (*Dei Verbum*),
- Pastoral Constitution on the Church in the Modern World (*Gaudium et Spes*).

Nine are decrees:

- Decree on the Apostolate of the Laity (*Apostolicam Actuositatem*),
- Decree on the Appropriate Renewal of the Religious Life (*Perfectae Caritatis*),
- Decree on the Bishops' Pastoral Office in the Church (*Christus Dominus*),
- Decree on the Church's Missionary Activity (*Ad Gentes*),
- Decree on Eastern Catholic Churches (*Orientalium Ecclesiarum*),
- Decree on Ecumenism (*Unitatis Redintegratio*),
- Decree on the Instruments of Social Communication (*Inter Mirifica*),
- Decree on the Ministry and Life of Priests (*Presbyterorum Ordinis*),
- Decree on Priestly Formation (*Optatam Totius*).

Three are declarations:

- Declaration on Christian Education (*Gravissimum Educationis*),
- Declaration on the Relationship of the Church to Non-Christian Religions (*Nostra Aetate*),
- Declaration on Religious Freedom (*Dignitatis Humanae*).

A Cathedral of Ideas

Unfortunately just thumbing through the constitutions, decrees, and declarations of Vatican II can be an intimidating experience, especially if you are unfamiliar with the technical language of theology and the distinctive style of official Church publications. Actually trying to read the documents can be even more frustrating. Like the Bible, they can deflect the best intentions of the earnest would-be reader.

When I was a Baptist college student in the 1970s, I had the good fortune of running across a little book called *Meet the American Catholic*. Designed for a Protestant audience, it compared the Catholic tradition to a "large and sprawling building"—the spiritual home to then about half a billion people (Scharper 5). The author, a prominent Catholic journalist, guided the reader through the vast house of Roman Catholicism floor by floor and room by room. He admired the ancient foundations, pointed out new wings and renovation projects, and paused especially to explain the significance of the house's well-stocked library (the Church's appreciation for things of the mind) and its spacious dining room (the eucharistic heart of the Catholic life). Chapter after chapter, I entered more deeply into the mystery of the Church. Thanks to the author's creative use of the concrete image, I began to think about the "house of God" (Hebrews 10:21) in a way that eventually led me to seek the fullness of Christianity in the Catholic tradition.

We will take a similar approach in this book. Almost everyone has seen photographs of the world's great cathedrals. Some of us have even been lucky enough to visit the sites and kneel where generations of saints and martyrs have prayed. Notre Dame in France, Santiago de Compostela in Spain, Saint Patrick's in New York City, Saint John Lateran in Rome, the pope's cathedral and the "mother church" of Christendom—these are treasures of Catholic civilization. They are more than marvels of art and engineering, though. In a language of symbol and figure inherited from ancient Israel and perfected in Christian Europe, they communicate to us a wisdom that transcends time and place.

The Catholic cathedral, as novelist Victor Hugo once said, is a "bible of stone" (200). Enter a cathedral and you see the Gospel in 3-D. Images of angels and apostles surround us. Scenes of heaven and hell transport us to worlds unknown. Soaring height and haunting shadow set before our eyes the full grandeur of God's redemptive drama. Even the cruciform (cross-shaped) floor plan declares through the magic of expert masonry the "plan of the mystery hidden for ages" (Ephesians 3:9).

Some theologians have compared the works of Bonaventure, Thomas Aquinas, and Dante to the glories of a Gothic cathedral (see Balthasar II:18, III:13). In their own way, the documents of Vatican II also constitute a great cathedral—a cathedral of ideas. They, too, speak in a language rich in faith, a language shaped by the biblical world view and centuries of spiritual experience. Enter them and you will be struck by a climate of holiness. Learn their special grammar and vocabulary, and what seems to be overwhelming complexity will give way again and again to the "simplicity that is in Christ" (2 Corinthians 11:3, Douay-Rheims). View them from above, and you will recognize the cathedral's characteristic cruciform pattern. Christ, in other words, is the core message of the Second Vatican Council—as Pope Paul VI said, "Christ who is both the road we travel and our guide on the way" (*Council Speeches* 19–20).

The Plan of This Book

Imagine, then, the documents of Vatican II as a vast cathedral of paragraphs and footnotes. We will begin our study at its altar, the focal point in any Catholic church. A careful reading of the council's first document, the Constitution on the Sacred Liturgy, will set the tone for our investigation into Vatican II's overall meaning and significance. Next, we will turn to the cathedral's ambo or pulpit, the place for the reading and proclamation of the word of God. Here we will examine the council's Dogmatic Constitution on Divine Revelation. After that, we will move on to the *cathedra*, the bishop's chair, and into the nave, the main body of the structure where the people of God assemble in all their diversity. Chapters on the Dogmatic Constitution on the Church and the documents dealing with Catholic identity, vocation, and ministry will show us why Vatican II has rightly been called the most Church-centered council in Christian history. In the final two chapters, we will look back through the nave and head toward the cathedral's great door. Here the people of God enter the world and engage it in service, participating in God's work of "reconciling the world to himself" (2 Corinthians 5:19). The book concludes with an analysis of some of the most memorable texts produced by any council: the Pastoral Constitution on the Church in the Modern World and the documents on topics such as Christian unity, religious freedom, and interfaith dialogue.

Before we begin our exploration of the council records, however, we should get better acquainted with the event of Vatican II itself. We need to see how this cathedral of ideas was designed and how its construction was organized and executed. Like the great cathedrals of Christendom, the Second Vatican Council was the result of massive—even heroic—group effort. From monks to stonemasons, the medieval cathedral builders were men of extraordinary brilliance and skill working in an age of unquestioned faith. The fathers of the Second Vatican Council exhibited a similar kind of genius, but with one major difference: "Living stones" themselves (1 Peter 2:5), they erected a monument of faith in an age when many thought faith had no future.

CHAPTER ONE

The Story of Vatican II

The Second Vatican Council was the twenty-first major council in the history of the Catholic Church. Official meetings of the Church's bishops, known as ecumenical councils (from the Greek *oikoumene*, the "whole world"), have punctuated the Catholic story for centuries. They have their roots in the meetings of the original apostles, who made world-changing decisions based on what "seemed good to the Holy Spirit and to us" (Acts 15:28).

Always named after the city in which they were held, ecumenical councils have usually been called to address a problem of heresy (false doctrine) or respond to a threat of schism (division in the Church). Sometimes they have been called to declare or clarify a core teaching of the faith.

The concept of councils is based on the distinctively Catholic understanding of the Church. The Church is not a human organization of like-minded individuals. It is a one-of-a-kind institution established by divine mandate and endowed with apostolic authority. Christ promised that the Holy Spirit would guide his Church "into all the truth" (John 16:13). Over two millennia, councils have played a major role in discovering and declaring that truth.

The Council of Nicea (AD 325) was the first ecumenical council. The Nicene Creed emerged out of its deliberations. Other important councils include Constantinople (381), Ephesus (431), and Chalcedon (451). These meetings completed the job of Nicea and defined the cardinal mysteries of the Holy Trinity and the Incarnation (the *Logos* or Word of God made flesh). Many councils later, Trent (1545–1563) defended

Catholic tradition against the challenges of the Protestant Reformation, and Vatican I (1869–1870) proclaimed the dogma of papal infallibility.

Vatican II was the most recent council in the historic series and the largest of all time. Some 2,500 bishops gathered in Vatican City's Basilica of Saint Peter's during four sessions (each roughly four months long) from the fall of 1962 to Advent in 1965. The bishops were assisted by nearly 400 priest-theologians (called *periti* or expert advisors) and energized by the presence of more than 150 special guests—auditors representing the Catholic faithful (lay people and women religious) and observers from Eastern Orthodox and Protestant traditions. Scores of reporters and untold numbers of pilgrims and tourists also participated in the event.

Blessed John XXIII, the pope who convened Vatican II, urged his fellow bishops to make the meeting a "wonderful spectacle of truth, unity, and charity" (*Ad Petri Cathedram*, 62). Eyewitnesses spoke of it as a new Pentecost. Today we recognize Vatican II as a crucial turning point for generations of Catholics and much of the non-Catholic world. Many historians call it the most important religious event of the twentieth century.

Preparation for the Council:
1959-1962

Pope John publicly revealed his intent to call a council on January 25, 1959, the feast of the Conversion of Saint Paul. He broke the news to a small group of cardinals at Rome's Basilica of Saint Paul Outside the Walls. The pope spoke of two "spectacles" in modern society that spurred him to action: the growth of materialism and unbelief in the secular world and the rise of a new confidence in the Catholic community. In response to these developments, he declared, he would initiate three major projects during his pontificate: (1) a special assembly or synod for the leaders of the diocese of Rome, (2) a revision of canon (Church) law, and (3) an ecumenical council. The Italian word chosen to characterize the canon law project—*aggiornamento* (updating)—soon became the unofficial motto for the larger project of the council, too.

On Pentecost 1959, John started the preparation for Vatican II by appointing a special commission comprising members of the Vatican administration called the Roman Curia. The commission sent questionnaires to thousands of bishops, theologians, and heads of religious orders, seeking input on issues that needed to be addressed at the council.

A year later, the pope established ten commissions to set the council's agenda. The commissions focused on subject areas such as theology, missions, and sacraments, and began to generate position papers for the council's consideration. Pope John also created the Secretariat for Promoting Christian Unity, today the Pontifical Council for Promoting Christian Unity, one of the Vatican's most important departments.

Pope John formally announced the Church's twenty-first ecumenical council on Christmas Day 1961. In his apostolic constitution *Humanae Salutis*, he called upon the entire Catholic world to read the "signs of the times" (Matthew 16:3), pray for a new outpouring of the Spirit, and work for "a better day for the Church and for mankind." Then, he made it all official: "We announce, We proclaim, We convoke, for this coming year of 1962, the second Sacred Ecumenical and universal Council of the Vatican" (*Encyclicals* 387, 393).

The First Session:
1962

Each session of the council included a staggering amount of business. Hundreds of hours were devoted to speeches, debates, the writing and rewriting of texts, and the process of consensus building. The council also included great pageantry. Imagine the procession through Saint Peter's Square: the long line of bishops in full regalia, along with the Bishop of Rome carried on the *sedia gestatoria*, the portable papal chair. Opening and closing ceremonies often lasted for hours. Everything was in Latin—the documents, the liturgies, even the speeches.

The first session began on October 11, 1962, then the feast of the Maternity of the Blessed Virgin Mary, now Blessed John's feast day. The

Holy Father's opening speech articulated his vision for the extraordinary event. The task of faith, he said, means discerning how to live the Gospel in our own time. He recognized the problems plaguing modern experience but refused to see only evil in contemporary society. The modern world offered the body of Christ a terrific challenge but also a tremendous opportunity.

John defined the main objective of the council as evangelical (Gospel-centered) and its basic orientation as pastoral. Proclaim the Gospel to an anxious world, he encouraged the fathers, and do so with the "medicine of mercy." Divine revelation never changes, but new modes of expression may be necessary if the secular world is to encounter Christ and if the Church is to embrace anew her high calling. The pope made it clear that Vatican II would be different from all other councils. It would not condemn a new heresy or define a new dogma. Its aim would be more general: to raise the "torch of religious truth" and show the Church to be the "loving mother of all" (Abbott 716).

The first document the council released was a semiofficial statement called "Message to Humanity" (often omitted from collections of the Vatican II texts). In just over 1,000 words, the bishops identified the Church's main mission as service to the world "so loved" by God (John 3:16). Renewing the Church, the fathers declared, meant solidarity with the poor and defense of human dignity. The message was especially noteworthy for its outreach to other faiths: "We humbly and ardently call for all men to work along with us in building up a more just and brotherly city in this world" (Abbott 6).

For the rest of the first session, the bishops began their evaluation of the documents submitted by the commissions. They voted on draft documents called *schemata* or *schemas* and then voted on the final versions. Every text required a two-thirds majority approval to become part of the Church's magisterial teaching.

The *schema* on revelation exposed the greatest degree of division among the fathers during the first session. Many thought its talk of "two sources" of revelation, Scripture and tradition, simply repeated slogans from the Reformation era and did not take seriously new perspectives in biblical studies. The pope intervened in the debate, directed two committees to work together on a new text, and encouraged the fathers to move forward.

John concluded the session on December 8, the feast of the Immaculate Conception. Weakened by cancer, he commended the bishops for their hard work and encouraged them to prepare for the long road ahead: "Then, doubtless, will dawn that new Pentecost which is the object of our yearning" (*Encyclicals* 444).

The Second Session:
1963

"Good Pope John" died on Pentecost Monday, June 3, 1963. The new pope, Paul VI, made it clear that Vatican II would be the top priority of his papacy. He convened the second session on September 29, 1963, the feast of Saint Michael the Archangel. In his opening address, he identified four key goals for the council: (1) reexamination of the nature of the Church, (2) renewal of the Church's self-awareness, (3) advocacy of Christian unity, and (4) promotion of dialogue with the contemporary world. Above all, he said, the council must present Christ as the answer to the questions of the modern age (*Council Speeches* 22).

The second session's work revolved around the *schema* on the Church. Discussion became heated as the bishops tackled issues dealing with specific offices and ministries. Two topics in particular occupied the fathers.

The first was the collegiality of bishops, the mutual respect for and common work of the apostles' successors. The individual bishop's authority in his own diocese is one thing, but what about his connection with his colleagues? What about the authority of the college, or brotherhood, of bishops as a whole? And how does this body relate to the pope?

The second topic was the proposal to reestablish the institution of the permanent diaconate (the order of deacons). In the early Church, deacons occupied a distinct position of service, not a transitional step toward priesthood. What made the idea especially controversial at

Vatican II was the proposal to ordain married men to the office (see 1 Timothy 3:12).

By the beginning of Advent, it was clear that the council would continue for at least one more session. A welcome sign of success was its approval of two completed documents: the Constitution on the Sacred Liturgy and the Decree on the Instruments of Social Communication. Statements on more sensitive issues such as Christian unity and religious liberty would have to wait for another day.

Pope Paul concluded the session on December 4, the feast of Saint Peter Chrysologus and Saint Barbara. He publicly embraced the ideal of collegiality, referring to himself simply as "Paul, Bishop of the Catholic Church." The high point of the ceremony was the pope's announcement of his plan to visit the Holy Land after Christmas. Along with future trips to south Asia, the Americas, Africa, and Australia, this papal pilgrimage vividly reinforced Vatican II's new attitude of openness toward the world.

The Third Session:
1964

Paul's journey portrayed on the world's stage the core values of the council. His cordial meeting in Jerusalem with Eastern Orthodox leader Athenagoras, Patriarch of Constantinople, underscored his commitment to Christian unity. His first encyclical, *Ecclesiam Suam* (1964), also advanced council themes. Its image of four concentric circles of dialogue—with the world, with non-Christian religions, with non-Catholic Christians, and within the Catholic community itself—established dialogue as a permanent part of magisterial teaching. The pope's founding of the Vatican Secretariat for Non-Christians, later renamed the Pontifical Council for Interreligious Dialogue, launched the Church into the uncharted waters of interfaith encounter.

During the third session, a backlog of *schemas* demanded a more rapid pace of deliberation. Three were approved: the Decree on Eastern Catholic Churches (Eastern-rite Churches in communion with Rome), the Decree on Ecumenism (now using "ecumenical" to refer to the unity of Catholics with all Christians), and the Dogmatic Constitution on the Church. The ideas expressed in these texts, especially references to the Church as the "people of God" and the "Pilgrim Church," profoundly influenced the emerging theological outlook of the other documents still in committee.

A slate of new *schemas* addressed all sorts of topics: the reform of religious life, the formation of priests, the ministry of bishops, the vocation of the laity, missionary work, and Christian education. Proposed declarations on religious liberty and the Church's relationship to non-Christians exposed more divisions among the bishops. Critics of the religious liberty text thought it contradicted previous Church teaching on church-state matters. Bishops from the Middle East feared that an overly positive statement on Judaism would endanger Catholics in Arab countries.

A new document called *Schema 13* also stimulated debate. It covered a broad array of subjects dealing with modern life—from marriage to nuclear war. Eventually it would become the Pastoral Constitution on the Church in the Modern World, one of the council's best-known publications.

By far, the most important text that returned to the assembly was the previously tabled document on revelation. As it evolved through one revision after another, it placed more and more emphasis on biblical studies in Catholic theology and the Bible in Catholic spirituality.

Pope Paul played an increasingly prominent role as the session proceeded. He postponed a vote on the religious liberty document, fearing the escalation of conflict, and appointed a special commission to review the question of artificial birth control. Committed to the council's call to reclaim the simplicity of the Gospel, he placed his silver tiara on the altar of Saint Peter's and never again wore the famous "triple crown." At the conclusion of the session, he announced a new title for the Blessed Virgin Mary: *Mater Ecclesiae*, "Mother of the Church" (*CCC* 963).

The Final Session:
1965

Vatican II's fourth session was its longest, its most productive, and its last. The Exaltation of the Cross (September 14) and the feast of the Immaculate Conception (December 8) served as bookends for the council's closing act. The session's ceremony, like its workload, was at peak level. Something as simple as the pope's decision to enter Saint Peter's on foot, retiring the *sedia gestatoria*, powerfully communicated a spirit of new beginnings.

Paul's contributions to the final session shaped the course of discussion on the council floor and the outcome of the council as a whole. He endorsed the idea of a synod of bishops meeting regularly after the council and committed himself to the reform of the Roman Curia. He also started the beatification process for his predecessors Pius XII and John XXIII. A trip to the United States, featuring a speech before the United Nations and a Mass at Yankee Stadium, greatly boosted international interest in the council.

Most of the fourth session was devoted to the final debates on the remaining texts. The fathers approved a total of eleven documents: six decrees on the ministry of bishops, the renewal of religious life, the training of priests, the ministry of priests, the lay apostolate, and the Church's missionary activity; three declarations on education, religious liberty, and world religions; and two constitutions: the Dogmatic Constitution on Divine Revelation and the revised version of *Schema 13*, the Pastoral Constitution on the Church in the Modern World.

The Close of the Council

Vatican II concluded as the Church entered another Advent season. Long processions lined Saint Peter's Square, and pilgrims poured into the Eternal City. Three days were set aside for the final ceremonies.

On December 4, again the feast of Saints Peter Chrysologus and Barbara, the bishops and the non-Catholic observers met for an ecumenical service at the place where Pope John had started it all: Saint Paul's Outside the Walls. The feast of Saint Ambrose, December 7, brought another unparalleled event. Pope Paul and Patriarch Athenagoras—at coordinated proceedings in Rome and Istanbul, Turkey—simultaneously lifted the sentences of excommunication that had separated their Churches since the East-West Schism of 1054.

Paul reminded the assembly just how unusual Vatican II's orientation had been. Never before had a council focused so intently on the nature and mission of the Church. Never before had a council concentrated so generously on the human experience. "Yes, the Church in Council has been concerned," he said, "not only with herself and her relationship with God, but also with man—man as he really is today" (Galli 289).

The next day, December 8, the feast of the Immaculate Conception, the final ceremony was held outdoors. Thousands crowded the piazza of Saint Peter's. Thousands more followed the events on radio and television. The Holy Father placed the council in the broadest possible context: "From this Catholic center of Rome, no one, in principle, is unreachable; in principle, all men can and must be reached. For the Catholic Church, no one is a stranger" (*Homily of Pope Paul VI*, paragraph 4).

The Legacy of Vatican II

An ecumenical council is a milestone in any period of Christian history. Vatican II's significance in the modern Catholic story cannot be overstated. Its directives dramatically changed longstanding attitudes and patterns of behavior in the international Catholic community. A simplified liturgy in the language of the people was only one sign of its impact. The twenty-first ecumenical council sparked a full-scale review of virtually every aspect of Catholic life and thought. Vatican II defines the way to be Catholic in the contemporary world.

The council, however, was not just an experience for one or two generations. Identifying it too closely with the 1960s and 1970s trivializes it. The council was timely, yes—a "providential" response to the trials of the twentieth century, as Blessed John Paul II once said (*Tertio Millennio Adveniente*, 18). But its voice has a timelessness all its own. Vatican II transcends the era of its origin and the first phase of its implementation. The encounter with its teachings has really only begun. After all, some 1,700 years later we are still trying to digest the insights of Nicea.

In the Great Jubilee Year 2000, John Paul, who served as one of the bishops at Vatican II, issued a call for fresh engagement with the council's documents: "*A new season is dawning before our eyes: it is time for deep reflection on the Council's teaching,* time to harvest all that the Council Fathers sowed and the generation of recent years has tended and awaited" (*Address to the Conference Studying the Implementation of Vatican II*, 9). Today, reflection on the council's wisdom is a driving force in Catholic experience. Memories of the event fade with time, and every year we lose more eyewitnesses. The documents of Vatican II, however, stand as testimony to what—in our own age—seemed good to the Holy Spirit and to us.

CHAPTER TWO

The Renewal of Catholic Worship

We begin our tour of Vatican II's cathedral of ideas at the altar, the link between our world and the eternal. Sacramental worship centered on the altar is the trademark of classical Catholic Christianity. *Sacrosanctum Concilium*, the council's Constitution on the Sacred Liturgy, reaffirms this cardinal feature of the tradition and reconfirms the Catholic faith's longstanding appreciation for art and beauty in Christian spirituality and human experience.

These themes run counter to the anti-institution and anti-ritual currents so prevalent in secular society today. The council document, approved in 1963, appeared just as a revolution of values was sweeping the modern world. The "worship wars" that have rocked the Catholic community for the last few decades—over issues such as music, architecture, inclusive language, and the proper posture for prayer—have never denied the basic human need to honor the Creator in ceremony and song. Catholics on all sides of the debate have always agreed on one fundamental point: Liturgy is vital to the Catholic way of life and human existence itself. Sadly, many of our non-Catholic neighbors cannot even understand what all the fuss is about. In complete sincerity they might ask, "Why worship at all?"

For the fathers of Vatican II, liturgy (from the Greek *leitourgia*, "public service" or "work of the people") was not just one idea among others. The "spirit and power of the liturgy" (*SC*14) was woven into the fabric of the council's purpose and practice. The council's schedule was designed to harmonize with the rhythm of the liturgical calendar. As we have seen, sessions opened and closed on major holy days, half of them feast days honoring the Virgin Mary. The Eucharist's prominent role made the whole council one great sacrifice of thanksgiving. Each of the four sessions began and ended with Mass. Bishops celebrated Mass every morning before attending to the day's agenda. The fathers showcased the Church's liturgical diversity and reintroduced the practice of concelebration—pope and bishops presiding at the altar together.

Constitution on the Sacred Liturgy

Sacrosanctum Concilium, Vatican II's Constitution on the Sacred Liturgy, was the first official document approved by the council, aside from the impromptu "Message to Humanity." The constitution's opening statement gives us the council's first articulation of its objectives: "The sacred Council has set out to impart an ever-increasing vigor to the Christian life of the faithful; to adapt more closely to the needs of our age those institutions which are subject to change; to foster whatever can promote union among all who believe in Christ; to strengthen whatever can help call all mankind into the Church's fold" (*SC* 1).

After a brief introduction, in which it affirms both the human and the divine dimensions of the Church, the constitution addresses seven main topics: (1) basic principles for the restoration and promotion of the liturgy, (2) the mystery of the Eucharist, (3) the other sacraments and the sacramentals (popular devotional practices), (4) the Divine Office (the Liturgy of the Hours), (5) the liturgical year, (6) sacred music, and (7) sacred art. The document's main concern is a "general restoration" of the liturgy (*SC* 21).

Most first-time readers find the text of the constitution very surprising. For many people, Vatican II means only one thing: dramatic, even traumatic, change in worship. Some even imagine that the council was called for the very purpose of rejecting the liturgical past—specifically leveling a negative verdict against the Mass endorsed by the Council of Trent, popularly known as the Tridentine Mass. We forget that the

Tridentine Mass, revised by Pope John in 1962, was the official rite celebrated during the council itself. John's apostolic constitution *Veterum Sapientia* (1962), praising Latin for its special service to Catholic life, is unknown to almost every Catholic today.

Source and Summit

What we find in *Sacrosanctum Concilium* is not hostility toward the Church's heritage at all. Rather we are treated with a stately hymn to the riches of sacramental worship. The liturgy is hailed as "the summit toward which the activity of the Church is directed...[and] the fount from which all her power flows" (*SC* 10; see *LG* 11). The Eucharist deserves special honor as the supreme source of divine grace. It is an earthly "foretaste" of heaven's eternal song of praise (*SC* 8), the cosmic liturgy mentioned especially in the Psalms and the New Testament books of Hebrews and Revelation (see Psalms 29, 103; Hebrews 12:22–24; and Revelation 4–5, 19:6–8). In sacramental worship, the constitution says, "God speaks to his people, and Christ is still proclaiming his Gospel. And the people reply to God both by song and prayer" (*SC* 33). Worship is "the voice of the Church...the whole mystical body publicly praising God" (*SC* 99). Liturgy is the lifeblood of the mystical body of Christ on mission in the world:

> *The liturgy daily builds up those who are in the Church, making of them a holy temple of the Lord, a dwelling-place for God in the Spirit, to the mature measure of the fullness of Christ. At the same time it marvelously increases their power to preach Christ and thus show forth the Church, a sign lifted up among the nations, to those who are outside, a sign under which the scattered children of God may be gathered together until there is one fold and one shepherd (SC 2).*

Restoration of the Liturgy

The document does call for the "restoration, progress, and adaptation" of Catholic liturgy in light of the conditions of contemporary culture (*SC* 24), but it keeps its recommendations on the level of basic principles. Liturgy should be simple, clear, and reverent. Local languages and modern art may be introduced as needed. So may the native music and cultural expressions of people in mission countries. Still, Latin "is to be preserved" (*SC* 36), Gregorian chant given "pride of place" (*SC* 116), and the pipe organ "held in high esteem" (*SC* 120). A "reverent silence" should enhance the atmosphere of worship (*SC* 30), and everything should be governed by "a noble simplicity" (*SC* 34) with no trace of "rigid uniformity" (*SC* 37).

The overall tone of the constitution is informed by respect for "sound tradition" and openness to modern conditions (*SC* 4). Some things in the liturgy can be changed, the constitution states, but others are divinely established and should never be altered. Only bishops working in harmony with the Bishop of Rome may revise the Church's liturgy. No one, not even a priest, may add to or subtract from the liturgy "on his own authority" (*SC* 22). "There must be no innovations unless the good of the Church genuinely and certainly requires them, and care must be taken that any new forms adopted should in some way grow organically from forms already existing" (*SC* 23).

Active Participation

Four special concerns run through the document. One is the emphasis on "full, conscious, and active participation" in worship (*SC* 14). This theme was the keynote of an international liturgical renewal movement that stretched from the 1800s to the 1950s. Pope Saint Pius X introduced the phrase "active participation" into Catholic thought with his instruction on sacred music, *Tra le Sollecitudini* (1903). Authentic Christian worship, the pope said, springs from a careful and attentive sharing in the Church's mysterious sacramental life.

The Vatican II fathers made active participation the centerpiece of their theology of liturgy. Worship without the investment of the

whole person, they insisted, is not worthy of the name. "The Church...
earnestly desires that Christ's faithful, when present at this mystery
of faith, should not be there as strangers or silent spectators. On the
contrary, through a good understanding of the rites and prayers they
should take part in the sacred action, conscious of what they are doing,
with devotion and full collaboration" (SC 48).

Modern Needs

A related theme is the conviction that people in modern society have
lost the ability to appreciate ceremony and ritual. Modern opponents
of traditional religion speak of ritual with contempt, calling it a mean-
ingless relic from the unenlightened past. Real religion, they say, is a
private experience requiring no external or formal expression. The
council fathers realized that the "circumstances of our times" (SC 79)
and the "conditions of modern life" (SC 88) make liturgical education
a challenging pastoral problem. In the context of the secular city, even
practicing Catholics need a clearer understanding of the meaning of
liturgical action and a more intelligible rationale for liturgy's place
in the spiritual life. Many of the post-Vatican II reforms in Catholic
liturgy stem from this assessment of the one-dimensional modern
person—tone-deaf, we might say, when it comes to the role of ceremony
and symbol in human experience.

Liturgy and Scripture

Another leading concern in the constitution is the intimate relationship between liturgy and the Bible. The Church inherited from the
Jewish synagogue the practice of reading Scripture not only in the
act of worship but as an act of worship in its own right. A major factor contributing to the Second Vatican Council was an international
movement promoting biblical scholarship and rediscovery of the
Bible's power and relevance in Catholic culture. The council fathers
were especially interested in making sure the Bible never appeared to
be an extra element artificially inserted into the program of worship.
"Sacred Scripture," they maintained, "is of the greatest importance in

the celebration of the liturgy." Any genuine renewal of the Church's liturgical life must foster a "warm and lively appreciation of sacred scripture" (*SC* 24) and open up more liberally the "treasures of the Bible" (*SC* 51).

Art and Worship

The constitution's accent on art also deserves attention. From the temple of ancient Israel to the choral Mass of the Baroque era, the "perfection of beauty" (Psalm 50:2) has ever been a characteristic of worship in the Judeo-Christian tradition. We have already seen how *Sacrosanctum Concilium* seeks to protect the status of Gregorian chant and the pipe organ and recognize the achievements of modern composers. It describes sacred music as first among the arts, designed for "the glory of God and the sanctification of the faithful" (*SC* 112). The document also reminds us that the visual arts—sculpture, painting, and architecture—are integral parts of the Church's response to the "infinite beauty of God" (*SC* 122). The Church is the "patron of the fine arts" (*SC* 122), and artists who serve her "are engaged in a kind of holy imitation of God the Creator" (*SC* 127). Discernment, however, must be cultivated and high standards honored. Objects dedicated for use in divine worship should be "worthy, becoming, and beautiful, signs and symbols of things supernatural" (*SC* 122).

After the Council

The objectives of Vatican II never included a radical overhaul of Catholic liturgical life. The Constitution on the Sacred Liturgy approved "restoration, progress, and adaptation" of worship (*SC* 24) but did not issue a blueprint for full-scale liturgical reform. Rediscovering the simplicity of ancient worship and adapting the rite to modern conditions only gradually became concerns of the council fathers and the Church's hierarchy. The liturgical changes most often associated with Vatican II were not specifically mandated by the council but entered Catholic life during its aftermath.

Too often the story of post-conciliar liturgical change is filtered through popular myth. History shows no general outcry against Latin, nor did massive change happen overnight. During and after the council, Church leaders experimented with modified liturgies, especially rites in vernacular languages. The council said nothing about priests' celebrating Mass *versus populum* ("facing the people") instead of *versus Orientem* ("facing East"—in ancient churches, literally the direction in which the people faced when praying toward the altar).

A slightly altered rite appeared in 1965. The real turning point, however, was Pope Paul's apostolic constitution *Missale Romanum* (1969). This document, along with a 1970 decree from the Vatican's Sacred Congregation for Divine Worship, established a completely revised Roman rite designed to preserve the "old" and make use of the "new" (*Cenam Paschalem*, 15). The principal architect of the rite was Vincentian priest (and later archbishop) Father Annibale Bugnini, head of the post-conciliar working group charged with designing a new liturgy and making it a reality in the Catholic world. A controversial figure still shrouded in mystery, he defended the new approach to liturgy in his nearly 1,000-page memoir titled *The Reform of the Liturgy, 1948-1975* (published in Italian in 1983 and in English in 1990).

Novus Ordo

The revised rite, known as the Mass of Paul VI or the *Novus Ordo* (new order) Mass, went into effect on the First Sunday of Advent 1969. The most noticeable features of the rite are now very familiar to Catholics worldwide: the use of local languages, the priest facing the people across a freestanding altar, a generous lectionary of Scripture readings, a biblically focused homily, Communion in the hand and in "both kinds" (bread and wine), an emphasis on liturgy as a community celebration, and the active participation of lay people. Everything was ordered to the theme of "adapting the Church to the needs of today's apostolate" (*Cenam Pashalem*, 12).

Paul VI's revised rite opened a whole new horizon for the Catholic liturgical imagination. Contemporary music, simplified vestments and worship spaces, a relaxed relationship between celebrant and people, and a general air of informality have come to be standard features of the Catholic liturgical experience. Respect for local cultures is also a hallmark of post-Vatican II worship. Lay people have especially flourished in their new vocations as cantors, lectors, eucharistic ministers, diocesan liturgical directors, and members of parish liturgy committees.

Unity and Division

To this day, though, liturgy is a source of both unity and division in the Catholic world. The process of implementing the revisions varied from place to place. So did the quality of the implementation and the level of understanding achieved on the part of individual bishops, priests, educators, and lay people. In many cases, the revisions were accompanied by undisciplined experimentation and an unplanned revolution in Catholic tastes. For years, critics have complained of liturgies held hostage to fads and heritage put at risk. They have also linked the revised rite to declining rates of Mass attendance, the vocations crisis, and open dissent from Church teaching.

Extreme critics reject the legitimacy of Vatican II itself. Most critics, however, have been loyal members of the Church committed to the essentials of the council. Mourning the loss of Latin and the fading grandeur of Catholic worship, they distinguish between what the council actually said and questionable experiments carried out in its "spirit." Pope Paul himself expressed second thoughts on the issue of language. "The introduction to the vernacular," he said in 1969, "will certainly be a great sacrifice for those who know the beauty, the power and the expressive sacrality of Latin. We are parting with the speech of the Christian centuries" (*Address to a General Audience*, 8).

Reform of the Reform

In recent years, Church leaders have called for a "reform of the reform"—a new liturgical movement to reclaim the true intentions of Vatican II. Pope John Paul II spoke out against a "misguided sense of creativity" in Catholic worship. He also authorized greater access to the traditional Latin Mass—by the 1990s, virtually unknown to a whole generation of

Catholics. "Liturgy," he declared, "is never anyone's private property, be it of the celebrant or of the community in which the mysteries are celebrated" (*Ecclesia de Eucharistia*, 52).

Pope Benedict XVI, who served as one of the leading *periti* at Vatican II, has made the revival of reverence and artistic standards in worship a signature concern of his pontificate. His apostolic letter *Summorum Pontificum* (2007) echoed John Paul's concerns and gave even more freedom to priests and laity devoted to the Tridentine Mass, now called the "extraordinary form" of the Roman rite. Benedict's support for the new English translation of *The Roman Missal*, introduced in 2011, has also enhanced Catholic attitudes toward worship. The Holy Father's basic principle has always been the continuity of Catholic history: "In the history of the liturgy there is growth and progress, but no rupture. What earlier generations held as sacred, remains sacred and great for us too" (Letter on *Summorum Pontificum*).

Today, the altar remains what it always has been—the very center of our experience as Catholic Christians. Vatican II's Constitution on the Sacred Liturgy continues to be the touchstone for every idea of authentic and vibrant worship. Full liturgical renewal may never be ours this side of heaven. As we are still discovering, it is part of the ongoing work of the pilgrim Church.

CHAPTER THREE

Revelation of the Living God

In this chapter, we turn from the cathedral's altar to the ambo. The ambo (from the Greek for "raised area") has been the principal site for the reading and proclamation of God's word since the earliest days of Christianity. As we have seen, the first document in Vatican II's cathedral of ideas, the Constitution on the Sacred Liturgy, stressed the essential role of the Bible in worship. It also underscored the importance of preaching. By means of the sermon or homily, the council fathers said, "the mysteries of the faith and the guiding principles of the Christian life are expounded from the sacred text during the course of the liturgical year. The homily, therefore, is to be highly esteemed as part of the liturgy itself" (*SC* 52). Like two hands joined together for prayer, the liturgy of the word and the liturgy of the Eucharist unite to form the Church's everlasting "sacrifice of praise" (Hebrews 13:15).

In the Dogmatic Constitution on Divine Revelation, the Vatican II fathers explored in greater detail the ways in which God speaks to the human family and in particular to the covenant people of Israel and the people of the new covenant in Christ. Called *Dei Verbum* (the "Word of God"), the document continues to emphasize the centrality of Scripture in Catholic belief and practice. It does not, however, limit its attention to the Bible, nor does it sanction a "Bible only" view of revelation. The Bible itself reminds us that God speaks in "many and various ways" (Hebrews 1:1). *Dei Verbum* opens up for the reader, as if unrolling an immense scroll, the epic panorama of God's communication with his creation.

Constitution on Revelation

Dei Verbum is one of Vatican II's greatest theological achievements. Some council documents seem dated by their association with the climate of the 1960s. Some appear too dominated by the theme of *aggiornamento* (updating). The Dogmatic Constitution on Divine Revelation stands on its own as a witness to one of the bedrock claims of Catholic truth. It offers us a concise, comprehensive, and durable statement of the "revelation of the mystery that was kept secret for long ages" (Romans 16:25).

Dei Verbum addresses six main topics: (1) divine revelation as the disclosure and discovery of God and his saving truth, (2) the process of the transmission of revelation, (3) the inspiration and interpretation of sacred Scripture, (4) the Old Testament and its enduring value, (5) the New Testament and its authenticity, and (6) the importance of the Bible in the life of the Church. The constitution highlights the great value of modern historical-critical research and the great need for informed Bible-centered piety in Catholic life. Its main focus, though, is on the special and uniquely verbal nature of God's relationship with humanity.

In an age that questioned and at times denied the existence of God, Vatican II affirmed not only belief in God but belief in a certain kind of God. The Catholic Church has always professed faith in a God who is personal and who communicates. *Dei Verbum* renews this testimony to the living God who spoke long ago to prophets and apostles and speaks to us today through his "living and active" word (Hebrews 4:12).

From Trent to Vatican II

The Vatican II fathers anchored their teaching on revelation in the Church's long heritage of reflection on the role of the word in God's work of creation and redemption, especially the inspired ("God-breathed") words of the Jewish and Christian sacred writings (see 2 Timothy 3:16 and 2 Peter 1:21). The Council of Trent defined the revealed Gospel as "the whole truth of salvation and rule of conduct...contained in written books and in unwritten traditions which were received by the apostles from the mouth of Christ himself, or else have come down to us, handed on as it were from the apostles themselves at the inspiration of the holy Spirit" (Tanner II, 663). The First Vatican Council also spoke of revelation as "contained in written books and unwritten traditions which were received by the apostles from the lips of Christ himself, or came to the apostles by the dictation of the holy Spirit, and were passed on as it were from hand to hand until they reached us" (Tanner II, 806).

Dei Verbum continues this emphasis on the various ways of God's communication and makes its own contribution to this living heritage of reflection. From the beginning, the constitution avoids the doctrine of *sola scriptura* (Latin for "only Scripture")—an idea well-known to modern Christians but completely absent from the literature of Christianity's first thousand years, including the Bible itself. *Dei Verbum* also steers clear of the two-source theory of revelation—a simplistic approach sometimes found in Catholic catechetical material that gives the impression that Scripture and tradition are distinct and unrelated channels of revelation.

What the constitution offers instead is a robust, multidimensional view of revelation. The Bible and tradition are not separate tracks delivering quantities of divine information. "Living" Scripture (*DV* 21) and "life-giving" tradition, along with the "living" teaching office of the Church (*DV* 8), interact with each other like organs in a complex bodily system. As three forces in one divine process, Scripture, tradition, and the Church's magisterium cooperate dynamically to make the person of God and the truth of God—both God himself and his "eternal decrees" of salvation (*DV* 6)—vibrant realities in the lives of creatures stamped with the image of God.

"Handing On"

Tradition is the lifeblood of classical Christianity. Saint Paul used the Greek term *paradosis* ("handing on") when addressing the deepest mysteries of the Christian message. He introduced his narrative of the Last Supper with these unforgettable words: "For I received from the Lord what I also handed on to you..." (1 Corinthians 11:23; see 1 Corinthians 11:2, 15:3 and 2 Thessalonians 2:15, 3:6). Soon the Latin parallel *traditio* entered the Catholic vocabulary, and tradition became the unmistakable sign of the Catholic way of being Christian. We speak of Catholicism as a "religion of the book" only with qualifications. Before anyone conceived of a New Testament, God's word was transmitted to the world through the process of *paradosis*. An extraordinary band of apostles, prophets, evangelists, pastors, and teachers (Ephesians 4:11) handed on what they in turn had received.

Teaching Authority

Here we see how closely tradition is related to teaching authority. Christ granted the apostles "power and authority" (Luke 9:1), the right to "bind" and "loose" (Matthew 18:18), and the ability to forgive and retain sins (John 20:23). He especially authorized them to teach, promising to be with them "to the end of the age" (Matthew 28:20) and to guide them "into all the truth" (John 16:13). New Testament references to the "apostles' teaching" (Acts 2:42), the "standard of sound teaching" (2 Timothy 1:13), and the faith "once for all entrusted to the saints" (Jude 3), along with repeated warnings about "strange teachings" (Hebrews 13:9), show us how highly teaching authority was valued in the early Church. The "household of God," as Paul said, is built on the "foundation of the apostles and prophets" (Ephesians 2:19–20). Divinely ordained teaching authority made a canon of Scripture a possibility and private interpretation of Scripture a theological dead end (see 2 Peter 1:20).

Scripture, Tradition, Magisterium

Two passages in *Dei Verbum* pull these distinctively Catholic themes together. Section 9 describes the interdependence of Scripture and tradition:

> *Sacred Tradition and sacred Scripture...are bound closely together, and communicate one with the other. For both of them, flowing out from the same divine well-spring, come together in some fashion to form one thing, and move towards the same goal....Thus it comes about that the Church does not draw her certainty about all revealed truths from the holy Scriptures alone. Hence, both Scripture and Tradition must be accepted and honored with equal feelings of devotion and reverence.*

Section 10 highlights the way in which Scripture and tradition are interlaced with real apostolic authority on earth:

> *[T]he task of giving an authentic interpretation of the Word of God, whether in its written form or in the form of Tradition, has been entrusted to the living teaching office of the Church alone. Its authority in this matter is exercised in the name of Jesus Christ. Yet this Magisterium is not superior to the Word of God, but is its servant. It teaches only what has been handed on to it....It is clear, therefore, that, in the supremely wise arrangement of God, sacred Tradition, sacred Scripture, and the Magisterium of the Church are so connected and associated that one of them cannot stand without the others.*

The Role of Reason

For all its emphasis on the revealed word, *Dei Verbum* does not overlook the role of reason in our relationship with God. The constitution acknowledges the possibility of natural knowledge of God—knowing God "through the things he has made" (Romans 1:20). After all, the

Greek term *Logos*, so fundamental for our understanding of Christ (John 1:1-14), means not only "word" but also "reason"—an idea linked to the Old Testament concept of wisdom (see Proverbs 8, Wisdom 9). Here the council fathers deliberately went against the grain of the modern mind. Since the 1600s, Western culture has increasingly confined reason to the scientific method. Reason, many modern thinkers tell us, is powerless to reach beyond the realm of the senses.

Drawing from Vatican I's Dogmatic Constitution on the Catholic Faith, the bishops of Vatican II reaffirmed the Church's longstanding appreciation for what is traditionally known as natural theology. Humans can truly know their Creator without supernatural assistance: "God, the first principle and last end of all things, can be known with certainty from the created world, by the natural light of human reason" (*DV* 6).

Pope John Paul II echoed *Dei Verbum*'s respect for reason in his landmark encyclical *Fides et Ratio*, issued thirty-three years after the council: "Faith and reason are like two wings on which the human spirit rises to the contemplation of truth" (Introduction). The *Catechism of the Catholic Church* devotes a section to the same conviction (*CCC* 36–38). The harmony between reason and revelation has also been the mainspring of Benedict XVI's theological imagination.

Development of Doctrine

One of *Dei Verbum*'s special contributions to Catholic teaching is its endorsement of the concept of doctrinal development. The idea goes back to Blessed John Henry Newman, the famous convert-cardinal of the 1800s, and his *Essay on the Development of Christian Doctrine* (1845). Newman saw the Christian faith not as a static set of ideas embedded in a text but as a dynamic current of insights expanding over time. The Church, he said, is like the Virgin Mary, who "treasured all these things in her heart" (Luke 2:51). The apostles proclaimed the Gospel in its essentials. Uniquely Catholic teachings such as purgatory and the Immaculate Conception, not explicitly mentioned in the Bible, were present in seed form in early Christian preaching and devotion. Over the centuries, the Church has nurtured its understanding of revelation, finding ever more effective ways of communicating and comprehending the timeless truths of the message.

The principle of doctrinal development gained widespread acceptance in the years leading up to Vatican II. Newman, in fact, is hailed as one of the council's "absent fathers." The Dogmatic Constitution on Divine Revelation reflects his understanding of the dynamism of the Church's faith, ever growing and expanding, always aiming toward the fullness of truth:

The Tradition that comes from the apostles makes progress in the Church, with the help of the Holy Spirit. There is a growth in insight into the realities and words that are being passed on.... Thus, as the centuries go by, the Church is always advancing towards the plenitude of divine truth, until eventually the words of God are fulfilled in her....God, who spoke in the past, continues to converse with the spouse of his beloved Son. And the Holy Spirit, through whom the living voice of the Gospel rings out in the Church—and through her in the world—leads believers to the full truth, and makes the Word of Christ dwell in them in all its richness...(DV 8).

The Soul of Theology

Most of all, *Dei Verbum* seeks to reenergize Catholic engagement with the Bible. Modern study of the text is encouraged, especially critical analysis of the human elements in Scripture: the unique life situation, literary style, mindset, and intention of each biblical writer. At the same time, the constitution reaffirms traditional features of Catholic doctrine: the divine authorship of Scripture, the unity of the Old and New Testaments, and the Bible's accuracy and reliability, especially regarding what Jesus "really did and taught" (*DV* 19). Scripture "firmly, faithfully and without error" teaches the truth necessary for salvation (*DV* 11). It is the "very soul of sacred theology" (*DV* 24; see *OT* 16).

Ambo and Altar

Since Vatican II, rediscovery of the Bible has truly animated Catholic experience. Biblical study is now one of the most exciting areas of Catholic intellectual life, and Catholic scholars are undisputed leaders in the study of Jesus and his first-century context. The *Catechism of the Catholic Church*, saturated with scriptural references, has greatly enriched our sense of the tradition's biblical roots. Publications from the Pontifical Biblical Commission—on the historical truth of the Gospels (1964), biblical interpretation in the Church (1993), and Jewish currents in the Christian Bible (2001)—have also enhanced Catholic understanding of Scripture. Pope Benedict XVI, a world-class biblical theologian in his own right, opened a new chapter in the dialogue between faith and criticism with his two-volume *Jesus of Nazareth* (2007, 2011).

Nothing has had greater impact on Catholic appreciation of Scripture than the release of new Catholic translations of the Bible. English versions such as the *Jerusalem Bible* (1966), the *New American Bible* (1970, revised 2011), and the *New Jerusalem Bible* (1985) have delivered the latest biblical research to millions of ordinary believers. Many Catholic Bibles even include the text of *Dei Verbum* as a preface. Today, the Bible is the starting point and chief reference point for catechetical and theological instruction in Catholic parishes, schools, universities, and seminaries around the world.

All of that matters little, though, if Scripture is separated from life with God. Saint Jerome's maxim—"Ignorance of the Scriptures is ignorance of Christ" (*DV* 25)—is more than an invitation to academic investigation. The Church's Lord is not a character trapped in a text. No book can contain him (John 21:25). The true meaning of the Bible emerges only in the context of prayer and worship, where "dialogue takes place between God and man" (*DV* 25). Ultimately the Word of God is a person, not a book. Jesus is the "sum total of Revelation" (*DV* 2). We meet him in the words proclaimed from the ambo and kneel before his presence on the altar.

CHAPTER FOUR

The Revival of Catholic Identity

When we look up from the ambo and the altar, we see ranks of windows high above. Streams of light pour through stained glass, illuminating the shrine. The prologue to the Gospel of John connects the eternal Word of God, the *Logos*, with the phenomenon of light. He is the "true light" which enlightens every human being (John 1:9). *Dei Verbum*, Vatican II's Dogmatic Constitution on Divine Revelation, celebrates the indispensible role of divine light in the Christian life. Because of revelation, we can see the truth about God and the truth about ourselves. As the psalmist says, "In your light we see light" (Psalm 36:9).

Because of this light, we can also see each other—fellow followers of the incarnate Word, or "children of light," to use the language of both Jesus and Saint Paul (see John 12:36, Ephesians 5:8, and 1 Thessalonians 5:5). Revelation unveils not only the presence of God among us but also the reality and true identity of the Church. The Church is not simply the community that believes in mysteries. It is a mystery of faith itself, part of the content of revelation, an article of faith on par with the Trinity and the resurrection of the dead.

At this point in our study, we move from the sanctuary with its altar and ambo into the main body of the cathedral's structure. Called the nave, it is the central space of the house of worship where the people of God assemble to profess the faith and celebrate the liturgy. Its name comes from the Greek word for "ship," and even its shape suggests the form of an ancient sailing vessel. The early Fathers linked the Church to Noah's ark (see 1 Peter 3:20–21), and Christian art portrays the Church as the boat or bark of Peter the fisherman (see Luke 5:3, where Jesus teaches the crowds from Simon Peter's ship).

Vatican II's chief document on the Church, the Dogmatic Constitution on the Church, reminds us that the Church is a community on a great voyage. But that is only one part of the constitution's message. At the beginning, the document's emphasis is on the theme of light. Its Latin title makes this clear. *Lumen Gentium* means "light of the nations" or "light of the Gentiles." It is a key phrase in the Bible's story of salvation history. The Servant Songs of Isaiah, for example, call Israel's promised redeemer "a light to the nations" (Isaiah 42:6; see 49:6). Aged Simeon in the Temple, holding the infant Messiah in his arms, thanks the God of Abraham for allowing him to see "your salvation...a light for revelation to the Gentiles and for glory to your people Israel" (Luke 2:30, 32).

Lumen Gentium's first sentence shows us how the Vatican II fathers connected the doctrine of revelation with the doctrine of the Church: "Christ is the light of humanity; and it is, accordingly, the heart-felt desire of this sacred Council, being gathered together in the Holy Spirit, that, by proclaiming his Gospel to every creature (see Mark 16:15), it may bring to all men that light of Christ which shines out visibly from the Church" (*LG* 1). We are called into the "marvelous light" of Christ, and in this light we can discover who we truly are: "a chosen race, a royal priesthood, a holy nation, God's own people" (1 Peter 2:9).

Constitution on the Church

Vatican II was the most Church-centered council in Christian history. It trained its sights on the uniquely modern question of how to be "children of light" in an era of rapid and radical social change. Pope Benedict has called the Church the "main theme of the entire Council" (*Theological Highlights of Vatican II*, 31).

At least ten of Vatican II's sixteen documents deal directly with ecclesiology, the branch of theology devoted to the study of the Church (*ekklesia* in Greek). They treat topics such as the structure, administration, ministries, and, more importantly, the personality and purpose of the Catholic Church. *Lumen Gentium* forms the nucleus of Vatican II's full-bodied ecclesiology. Like a mighty pipe organ filling the space of a cathedral with majestic music, it is the source of master ideas that reverberate through all the council documents. It is the document that best captures the council's basic insight into the Church, especially its uncommon call to the life of love and worship—the "deepest vocation of the Church" (*LG* 51). The constitution effectively highlights the overarching theme of the council: a Church empowered by its witness to timeless truth and strategically geared to the needs of the day.

The Church
as Sacrament

The Dogmatic Constitution on the Church is divided into eight sections: (1) The Mystery of the Church, (2) The People of God, (3) The Church is Hierarchical, (4) The Laity, (5) The Call to Holiness, (6) Religious, (7) The Pilgrim Church, and (8) Our Lady. The document begins by building on the council's document on liturgy. It continues and develops the eucharistic theme, describing the Church as a "sign and instrument... of communion with God and of unity among men" (*LG* 1). In one of its most memorable phrases, it declares the Church to be the "universal sacrament of salvation" (*LG* 48; see *AG* 1, 5 and *GS* 45).

In the sacraments, we use ordinary things such as bread, water, wine, oil, and even the human touch to help us discover the extraordinary presence of God in our lives. Built into the fabric of the Catholic world view is the seemingly audacious idea that a material thing can be the meeting ground for God and the human person, a carrier for divine grace. Our experiences of baptism, confirmation, confession, marriage, ordination, the anointing of the sick, and especially holy Communion—the "source and summit of the Christian life" (*LG* 11; see *PO* 5, 14)—teach us to put faith in what may be our tradition's most astonishing claim.

Catholicism's sacramental principle, however, goes far beyond the Church's standard seven rites, as beautiful and significant as they are. The sacramental world view sees all of creation as potentially a vehicle for God's revelation and redemptive activity. *Lumen Gentium* declares that the Church itself is one immense sacrament. We could picture it as the sacrament of all sacraments—a cosmic body of millions of human beings, transmitting grace to the world as it encircles the globe and spans the gap between the living and the dead.

Human and Divine

Like any sacrament, the Church has a double character. Its outer, natural dimension is a matter of public record. The Catholic Church is one of the most visible social institutions on earth. It can be, and routinely is, analyzed and scrutinized in news reports and history books. Many people see it as the epitome of organized religion, for better or for worse.

To discern the Church's inner, supernatural dimension, we have to enter into the realm of mystery. The mystical body of Christ is a spiritual fellowship of saints, saints-in-the-making, and even angels—an association that defies conventional categories. It is unlike any other family or group in all of history and all of creation.

Lumen Gentium declares that the visible Church and the invisible Church are not two separate entities. They represent two sides of "one complex reality" (*LG* 8). The Church is one. But we must also remember that it is holy, despite the sins of its members and leaders. The Church is both human and divine, founded by God himself. "For this reason," the constitution explains, "the Church is compared, in a powerful analogy, to the mystery of the incarnate Word" (*LG* 8).

Here we penetrate to the deepest level of the Church's mystery. God became man to reconcile the world to himself (2 Corinthians 5:19). That union and that reconciling mission live on in the life of the Church, described by Paul as the "fullness" of Christ himself (Ephesians 1:23). The Church is an extension of the Incarnation. As Christ's human nature served the divine Word in his mission of salvation, "so, in a somewhat similar way, does the social structure of the Church serve the Spirit of Christ who vivifies it, in the building up of the body" (*LG* 8).

Organic and Ordered

Lumen Gentium uses many other images to illustrate the mystery of the Church. Most come from the New Testament: a sheepfold, a flock, a field, a temple, a city, and personal images such as mother, body, and bride. Two images that sparked great enthusiasm in the years following the council are the "people of God" and the "Pilgrim Church." Both express the human, organic, and unfinished character of Christian experience—nicely complementing Newman's idea of doctrinal development. Both images especially honor the place of lay people in the community of faith. The constitution stresses the dignity of the "common priesthood of the faithful" (*LG* 10), the importance of the family as a "domestic Church" (*LG* 11), the laity's supernatural sense of the faith (*LG* 12), and the "wonderful diversity" that makes the Church truly "catholic" or all-encompassing (*LG* 32).

At the same time, the Church is an ordered community. Hierarchy (from the Greek for "holy rule" or "holy origin") is not a man-made component of its identity. All the structures of authority—including papal primacy, apostolic succession, ranks of ministry, the college of bishops, and councils—are permanently built into the Church's framework by divine design. The constitution is particularly careful to spell out the relationship between the pope and his fellow bishops:

> *The order of bishops is the successor to the college of the apostles in their role as teachers and pastors, and in it the apostolic college is perpetuated. Together with their head, the Supreme Pontiff, and never apart from him, they have supreme and full authority over the universal Church; but this power cannot be exercised without the agreement of the Roman Pontiff. The Lord made Peter alone the rock-foundation and the holder of the keys of the Church (see Matthew 16:18–19), and constituted him*

shepherd of his whole flock (see John 21:15 ff)....The supreme authority over the whole Church, which this college possesses, is exercised in a solemn way in an ecumenical council. There never is an ecumenical council which is not confirmed or at least recognized as such by Peter's successor (LG 22).

Unique But Inclusive

The most striking claims of *Lumen Gentium* concern the Church's uniqueness and its inclusive relationship with non-Catholic and non-Christian traditions. Christ founded one Church, the "pillar and bulwark of the truth" (1 Timothy 3:15). "This Church," the constitution states, "subsists in the Catholic Church, which is governed by the successor of Peter and by the bishops in communion with him" (*LG* 8). It is the divinely established agency necessary for the salvation of the human race:

[T]he one Christ is mediator and the way of salvation....He himself explicitly asserted the necessity of faith and baptism (see Mark 16:16; John 3:5), and thereby affirmed at the same time the necessity of the Church which men enter through baptism as through a door. Hence they could not be saved who, knowing that the Catholic Church was founded as necessary by God through Christ, would refuse either to enter it, or remain in it (LG 14).

Holiness and truth, however, can be found outside the visible Church and outside of Christianity altogether. Baptized Christians in non-Catholic communities are "joined in many ways" to the Church in communion with the Bishop of Rome (*LG* 15). Jews are "a people most dear" to God and to all true Christians. Muslims are also mysteriously related to the body of baptized disciples. So are those who "in shadows and images seek the unknown God" (see Acts 17:23). Salvation is possible for those "who, through no fault of their own, do not know the Gospel of Christ or his Church, but who nevertheless seek God with a sincere heart, and, moved by grace, try in their actions to do his will as they know it through the dictates of their conscience" (*LG* 16).

Still, we are bound by the Great Commission: "Go therefore and make disciples of all nations" (Matthew 28:19). The missionary spirit is permanently engraved on the heart of Christianity. Jesus Christ is the "source of salvation for the whole world" (*LG* 17). What is good in non-Christian religions, however, can serve as a "preparation" for his Gospel, thanks to the universal mission of the Holy Spirit (*LG* 16). Missionary activity, properly executed, does not destroy the good in non-Christian cultures but rather purifies and perfects it (*LG* 17).

The Call
to Holiness

Quickly it becomes clear that *Lumen Gentium* is no abstract exercise in ecclesiology. Its bold truth claims and its high view of the Church demand a response from even the casual reader. Cutting through the entire constitution is the biblical theme of decision: "Choose this day whom you will serve" (Joshua 24:15).

Vatican II awakened many Catholics for the first time to the dignity of their status as responsible moral agents and disciples of Christ. Today we realize that Christian morality can never be reduced to blind obedience to rule books or authority figures. Nor can discipleship be dismissed as the exclusive concern of a class of religious specialists. *Lumen Gentium*'s chapter on "The Call to Holiness" has played a major role in this transformation of consciousness: "All Christians in any state or walk of life are called to the fullness of Christian life and to the perfection of love" (*LG* 40).

"The Call to Holiness" is a miniature masterpiece of spiritual theology. It does not address particular moral issues or specific trials along the mystical way but keeps its aim on the ultimate goal of the spiritual life: participation in the divine nature (see 2 Peter 1:4). Its message is simple and startling. Vocation (from the Latin for "calling") is a question every Christian has to wrestle with, not just those called to the priesthood or the evangelical counsels of poverty and celibacy. We are all called to be saints.

In an era marked by confusion about the institution of marriage, we can especially profit from the chapter's section on family life. The sacrament of matrimony points to something far beyond itself. In the light of revelation, we see that even the ordinary things in life can be paths to an order marvelously transcending the boundaries of this world: "Christian married couples and parents...stand as witnesses and cooperators of the fruitfulness of mother Church, as a sign of, and a share in that love with which Christ loved his bride and gave himself for her" (*LG* 41).

Mary and the Church

One of the remarkable features of *Lumen Gentium* is its ability to personalize the Church. Too often we imagine the Church as a face-less crowd. Some commentators even speak of it in terms borrowed from James Joyce's experimental novel *Finnegans Wake*: "Here Comes Everybody" (32).

Catholic theology, however, typically leans the other way. Saint Paul emphasized the personality of the Church with his image of the body: "We who are many are one body" (1 Corinthians 10:17). In the second century, Saint Irenaeus referred to the Church as a single individual with a single soul. A thousand years later, Thomas Aquinas used similar language in his *Summa Theologiæ* (II-II, 83, xvi, 3). French philosopher Jacques Maritain, whose thought made a deep impression on Pope Paul VI, stated the same position in the era of Vatican II. The Church, he said, "is not only a people or a multitude, but also a supernaturally constituted common person who...believes as having a single heart, speaks as having but a single voice, acts as having but a single will..." (Maritain 17).

Lumen Gentium highlights this personal dimension of the Church in its final chapter on the Blessed Virgin Mary. Tradition has long associated Mary with Israel and the Church. Saint Luke includes her in his portrait of the earliest Christian community (Acts 1:14), and Christian art routinely locates her at the center of the apostolic circle on the day of Pentecost, the birthday of the Church.

Vatican II itself had a strong Marian orientation. It came on the heels of a Marian renaissance in modern Catholic life. The proclamation of the Immaculate Conception (1854) and the Assumption (1950) and apparitions including Lourdes (1858) and Fatima (1917) stimulated new interest in Mariology. As we have seen, Vatican II's sessions were timed to coincide with Marian feasts, and Pope Paul bestowed upon Our Lady the title of Mother of the Church.

Lumen Gentium contributes to this legacy by picturing Mary as the face of the universal Christian family:

> *The Church indeed contemplating [Mary's] hidden sanctity, imitating her charity and faithfully fulfilling the Father's will, by receiving the word of God in faith becomes herself a mother. By preaching and baptism she brings forth sons, who are conceived of the Holy Spirit and born of God, to a new and immortal life. She herself is a virgin, who keeps in its entirety and purity the faith she pledged to her spouse. Imitating the mother of her Lord, and by the power of the Holy Spirit, she keeps intact faith, firm hope and sincere charity.... Seeking after the glory of Christ, the Church becomes more like her lofty type...[Mary] is the image and beginning of the Church...* (LG 64, 65, 68).

Catholic spirituality has for centuries tied love of Mary to love of Christ: *Ad Jesum per Mariam* ("to Jesus through Mary"). Vatican II's Dogmatic Constitution on the Church concludes with a parallel mystery: the intimate relationship between Mariology and ecclesiology. In the nave of the cathedral, the people of God assemble in all their wonderful diversity. In the light of divine revelation, however, the Church's *everybody* looks strangely like *somebody*. To the eyes of faith, the council fathers said, this *somebody* is a woman full of grace.

CHAPTER FIVE

Catholic Ministry
and Vocation

Before we leave the metaphor of light, we should remind ourselves of one more thing: light comes in many different forms and degrees of intensity. The appearance of a cathedral depends greatly on whether we view it during the early Mass on Easter morning or the midnight Mass on Christmas Eve—or all alone on a quiet Saturday afternoon in summer. The Impressionist artist Claude Monet produced over thirty paintings of one of France's most cherished cathedrals during the 1890s. Each canvas in his *Rouen Cathedral* series captures the Gothic masterwork at a different time of day and a different place in the round of the seasons. Together they vividly show how variations in light affect our experience of objects in the natural world.

The same is true in the order of grace. Vatican II's documents portray the Church in various states of light and shade. What we saw in *Lumen Gentium* was the cathedral's nave bathed in moonlight and candlelight. The constitution's main topic, the "mystery of the holy Church" (*LG* 5), actually invites such a subtle and nuanced treatment. The council's shorter documents on ecclesiology—the decrees on special ministries and vocations—deal with the Church in a much more practical way. They show us the same nave, only now flooded with sunlight and the glow of electric lights.

Five of the council's decrees discuss pastoral renewal in particular forms of Church service and calling: the ministry of bishops, the formation and life of priests (a document on each topic), the gifts and responsibilities of religious life, and the apostolate or mission of lay people. These documents represent specific applications of the Constitution on the Church. Here we do encounter the "wonderful diversity" of the Church (*LG* 32), but it is still not a disordered *everybody*. What we discover is the structured and functional variety of a living and complex organism created for a specific purpose.

One Body, Many Gifts

Vatican II's ecclesiology is based largely on Saint Paul's image of the body—a brilliant analogy that works two ways. As we have seen, it powerfully communicates the unity of the Church. At the same time, it celebrates the role of multiple gifts in the life of the community. Many gifts, functioning harmoniously and energized by the Spirit, make the Church a dynamic force in the world.

In Paul's letters we see references to several types of leaders who exercised spiritual gifts in the early Church: apostles, prophets, evangelists, pastors, teachers, and more (see Romans 12:4–8, 1 Corinthians 12:4–30, and Ephesians 4:11–16). The New Testament also speaks of specific offices of authority: the *episkopos* (bishop), the *presbyteros* (elder or priest), and the *diakonos* (deacon). By the early second century, these positions defined the Church's emerging system of holy orders. The Apostolic Father Ignatius of Antioch, writing around the year 107, shows us in what high regard the offices were held by the first Christians: "You all should follow the bishop as Jesus Christ does the Father. Follow too the presbytery as the apostles, and honor the deacons as the command of God" (Howell 134). The Vatican II documents contribute to centuries of reflection on the Church's commitment to the *cura animarum* (the cure of souls). They fully endorse this "divinely instituted" system of Christian authority and the three ancient offices that historically have put it into practice (*LG* 28).

Bishops

A high view of the bishop's office is a prime feature of Catholic Christianity. The Bible places great emphasis on the qualifications for the *episcopacy* or the office of the bishop. Paul's letters to Timothy, bishop of Ephesus, and Titus, bishop of Crete, set the standard (see 1 Timothy 3:1–7 and Titus 1:7–9). The essence of the office, however, is much more than group management. A bishop is "made" by the Holy Spirit (Acts 20:28). His role is closely associated with the Savior's. Jesus is the supreme *episkopos* (1 Peter 2:25). Saint Ignatius instructed his readers to view their bishop "as the Lord himself" (Howell 79).

With Vatican II's Decree on the Bishops' Pastoral Office in the Church (*Christus Dominus*), we retrace our steps for a moment, turning back toward the altar of our cathedral of ideas. In the sanctuary, we skipped over one important item: the *cathedra* or bishop's chair. This piece of furniture, situated behind or beside the altar, is the one thing that makes a church a cathedral. It even gives the cathedral its name. In the ancient world, a chair was the sign of a teacher's authority (see Matthew 23:2), and to this day some professors occupy "chairs" in our universities. The *cathedra* is a concrete symbol of the bishop's authority as a successor of the apostles (*CD* 6). The Bishop of Rome, for example, is protected from error precisely when he proclaims the truths of salvation *ex cathedra*—"from the chair" of Peter the chief apostle.

The role of bishops in the Catholic Church has long been modeled on Christ's threefold office as prophet, priest, and king (*CCC* 436). Their mission, therefore, is to teach, sanctify, and govern the Good Shepherd's flock. *Christus Dominus* reaffirms this traditional three-part understanding of the bishops' mission while also seeking to make the ancient office responsive to the new order of things in modern society (*CD* 3). The decree's significance is only magnified when we remember that it is a message written and approved by the bishops of the world for the bishops of the world.

Christus Dominus places the teaching duties of the bishops in a missionary context. Bishops should be "witnesses of Christ to all men"—the baptized, those who have "strayed...from the path," and those "who have no knowledge of the gospel" (*CD* 11). They should proclaim the "whole mystery of Christ" (*CD* 12) and promote a living and active faith. Echoing Pope John's opening speech at the council, the decree challenges bishops to present Christian doctrine "in a manner suited to the needs of the times" (*CD* 13). Today's RCIA programs—implementing the Rite of Christian Initiation of Adults—have their roots in the decree's charge to upgrade the instruction of adult converts and inquirers (*CD* 14).

Bishops sanctify the Church through their celebration of the sacraments. They are the main dispensers of the mysteries of God and responsible for the quality and integrity of the liturgy in their churches. Holiness, however, can never be inspired simply by effective administration. To the priests, religious, and lay people in his diocese, the bishop must be an "example of sanctity in charity, humility and simplicity of life." He must also be an ardent promoter of vocations, especially to missionary work (*CD* 15).

Christus Dominus discusses the ruling function of bishops in terms of servant-leadership. Jesus measured true greatness on the scale of self-sacrifice: "I am among you as one who serves" (Luke 22:27). A bishop, therefore, must be "one who serves," and the range of his service is virtually unlimited. The decree locates non-Catholics, non-Christians, immigrants, and refugees within his circle of pastoral care. On the level of Church structure, it supports new organizational initiatives such as the establishment of national conferences of bishops and the modernization of the Roman Curia. The work of the United States Conference of Catholic Bishops—in education, evangelization, and social action—is a great example of how seriously Church leaders have heeded the voice of Vatican II (see www.usccb.org).

Priests

Ordained by bishops, who are priests themselves, priests bring the gifts of God to the people of God—from the altar and the ambo, deep into the heart of the nave. Catholicism without priesthood would not be Catholicism. From the beginning, the spread of the Church was accompanied by the appointment of presbyters or elders in every city (see Acts 14:23 and Titus 1:5). Paul labored in the "priestly service of the gospel of God" (Romans 15:16) and articulated the first benchmarks for this indispensable form of ministry (see 1 Timothy 5:17-22). The model of Christian priesthood is Christ himself: the "apostle and high priest of our confession" (Hebrews 3:1; see 5:10 and 6:20).

Vatican II's decrees on priesthood—both the Decree on Priestly Formation and the Decree on the Ministry and Life of Priests—tie the principal aim of the council to the integrity of priesthood in the Church: "The desired renewal of the whole Church depends in great part upon a priestly ministry animated by the spirit of Christ" (*OT* Introduction). Like bishops, priests participate in the threefold mission of Christ. The priesthood "builds up and sanctifies and rules" the body of Christ. Invested with a "special character" through ordination, priests are "configured to Christ the priest in such a way that they are able to act in the person of Christ the head" (*PO* 2). The "changed conditions of our times," however, require creative reflection on the theology and practice of priesthood (*OT* Introduction).

The decrees outline the proper preparation of candidates for the priesthood and frankly discuss those factors that will sustain an ordained man in his imitation of Christ. The decrees deal with the challenging pastoral responsibilities that confront the modern priest and the eucharistic lifestyle that best cherishes the "precious gift of priestly celibacy" (*PO* 16). The decrees especially concentrate on education. Priestly training should be grounded in Scripture, the "soul" of theology, as *Dei Verbum* said (*DV* 24). It should also include the study of Latin and the biblical languages, philosophy, the Church Fathers, modern social developments, and even the teachings of non-Catholic and non-Christian religions (*OT* 16). Priests in the modern world should be prepared not only to preach and teach but also to "enter into dialogue with their contemporaries" (*OT* 15).

The documents are at their best when they encourage priests to strive toward "that greater holiness that will make them daily more effective instruments for the service of all God's people" (*PO* 12). The stakes are high. Those who take up the priestly calling have the "hopes of the Church and the salvation of souls" in their hands (*OT* 22). The task of promoting priestly vocations, however, depends on all the faithful:

> *The duty of fostering vocations falls on the whole Christian community, and they should discharge it principally by living full Christian lives. The greatest contribution is made by families which are animated by a spirit of faith, charity and piety and which provide, as it were, a first seminary, and by parishes in whose abundant life the young people themselves take an active part* (OT *2).*

Priest Shortage, Ordination of Women?

Readers today may be surprised to see the documents address the issue of a priest shortage (see *OT* 6, *PO* 10, and *CD* 6). Since the council, a sharp decline in the number of active priests has become a major factor in everyday Catholic experience. Vatican II's response to the first signs of this trend invites us to keep the problem in supernatural perspective: "God will not allow his Church to lack ministers" (*OT* 6).

Contemporary readers may also be surprised to find no comment on the question of female ordination. The ordination of women became a topic of debate only in the 1970s, when some Protestant denominations abandoned traditional teachings on ministry and authority. Documents from the Congregation for the Doctrine of the Faith and the Pontifical Biblical Commission, released in 1976, confirmed the historic Catholic practice of restricting holy orders to qualified men. John Paul II issued the definitive statement in 1994: "The Church has no authority whatsoever to confer priestly ordination on women" (*Ordinatio Sacerdotalis*, 4).

Deacons

Another surprise for the first-time reader is the small amount of space devoted to the diaconate (from the Greek for "service"). Vatican II did not produce a decree on the third office of ministry mentioned in the New Testament and the Fathers (see Acts 6:1-6 and 1 Timothy 3:8-13). It did, however, survey the great range of the deacon's service—from liturgical leadership to the implementation of Catholic social teaching. More importantly, the council called for the reestablishment of the permanent diaconate and recommended opening the ministry to married men (*LG* 29; see *OE* 17). After the council, Paul VI outlined the standards for this ministry "always...held in great honor by the Church" (*Ad Pascendum*, Introduction). Today, over 36,000 men serve in the order (http://cara.georgetown.edu). The restoration of the permanent diaconate is one of the great success stories of Vatican II.

Religious

The three-tiered system of bishop, priest, and deacon gives Catholic ministry its well-known shape and character. It does not, however, offer a comprehensive picture of Catholic calling. The "wonderful diversity" of the Church, filling the nave of the cathedral, also includes men and women committed to the vocation of consecrated or religious life. For many centuries, this unique form of discipleship has exerted an enormous impact on virtually every aspect of civilization. Today, nearly one million religious priests, brothers, and sisters grace the Church and the world with their service (http://cara.georgetown.edu). They perform a "vital function" for the kingdom of God and enrich the people of God with their "great variety of gifts" (*PC* 1). Without religious life, Catholicism would be utterly unrecognizable—perhaps even nonexistent.

Religious life (from the Latin *religare*, "to bind") is a distinctive response to Christ's call to "be perfect" (Matthew 5:48). It is rooted in the evangelical counsels, the "hard sayings" of Jesus that accent voluntary poverty, celibacy, obedience, and nonviolence. Throughout Christian history, solitary hermits and members of various active and contemplative communities have aimed at such a higher righteousness (Matthew 5:20). Many have sought a countercultural lifestyle based on prayer "without ceasing" (1 Thessalonians 5:17). The essence of religious life is best expressed in the title of Thomas à Kempis' devotional classic: *The Imitation of Christ.*

We have already seen Vatican II's declaration of the universal call to holiness (*LG* 39–42). The council fathers were especially interested in reminding the Church that the evangelical counsels represent the ideal for every follower of Christ. The Church, they insisted, can never forget her "poor and suffering founder" (*LG* 8).

The Decree on the Appropriate Renewal of the Religious Life, *Perfectae Caritatis* ("Perfect Charity"), keeps the spotlight on the Christ-centered life. It advances the discussion of religious life initiated in *Lumen Gentium* (*LG* 43–47) and explores in greater depth a variety of issues related to the vocation—topics such as monasticism, missionary work, and the "life hidden with Christ in God" (*PC* 6).

Perfectae Caritatis is also concerned with institutional reform. Each religious community, it says, must rediscover the original spirit of its God-given mission and, at the same time, adapt its practice to the conditions of modern life. It even gets into the details of the modified religious habit—one of the most visible symbols of Vatican II's impact. The overall focus of the decree, though, is radical fidelity to Christ: "Before all else, religious life is ordered to the following of Christ... [E]ven the best-contrived adaptations to the needs of our time will be of no avail unless they are animated by a spiritual renewal" (*PC* 2).

Lay People

Vatican II's final decree on service and vocation completes our tour of the nave, the cathedral's great midsection. Its topic—the laity (from the Greek word *laos*, "people")—sets Vatican II apart from all other councils in Christian history. No other council has ever given so much and so positive attention to the role of lay people. According to the Decree on the Apostolate of the Laity, every baptized Catholic is a full member and a responsible member of "God's own people" (1 Peter 2:9).

The council's appreciation for the lay apostolate is one of its most distinctive features. An emphasis on the mission of lay people characterized Vatican II from the beginning. Early enthusiasm regarding "active participation" in the liturgy (*SC* 14) was a sign of more to come. *Lumen Gentium*'s sections on "The People of God" and "The Laity" celebrated the dignity of the "common priesthood of the faithful" (*LG* 10), the family as a "domestic Church" (*LG* 11), the laity's sense of the faith (*LG* 12, 35), and the "special vocation" of the laity to be the "salt of the earth" (*LG* 33). Laymen and women served as auditors at the council, and Vatican II was the first council in history to invite a lay speaker to address the assembly.

The council's Decree on the Apostolate of the Laity challenges conventional notions of lay responsibility. Catholic folklore reduces the layman's obligations to three: pray, pay, and obey. The decree sets a much higher standard. It links the lay disciple directly to the threefold task of the Savior: the "priestly, prophetical and kingly office of Christ" (*AA* 2). Lay people possess the "right and duty to be apostles" (*AA* 3). Their mission is the mission of the Church: to take Christ into the world. Lay people should participate in, and in some cases lead, the Church's work in education, evangelization, apologetics (defending the faith), and the "renewal of the temporal order" (*AA* 7). As believers and citizens, they should always be guided by a "single conscience, a Christian conscience" (*AA* 5) and should never become "slaves" of modern science and technology (*AA* 7). Male and female, young and old, married and single, all Catholics are invited to think creatively about their potential as "messengers of Christ" in the world (*AA* 14).

CHAPTER SIX

The Church and
the World

In the preceding chapters, we have explored major sections of Vatican II's cathedral of ideas. From its constitutions on liturgy, revelation, and the mystery of the Church to its five decrees on ministry and vocation, we have seen its altar, its ambo, its *cathedra*, its generous nave, and even its stained-glass windows. All of these features make up the cathedral's interior. Together they add up to an incomparable summary of the Gospel for the contemporary Catholic disciple.

Cathedrals, of course, also have exteriors. Often as elaborate as the finely crafted interior, the outer dimension of a cathedral constitutes the place where the Church touches the world. It is still a "bible of stone." Only now it is turned outward—a Gospel expressed in shapes and signs that even the nonbeliever can appreciate. What admirers of Monet's *Rouen Cathedral* paintings find so engaging, after all, is not the artist's portrayal of the structure's inner treasures but his treatment of its weather-beaten and war-scarred façade—the magnificent front or "face" of the church, well-known for its majestic towers and its massive portals or doorways depicting scenes from the history of salvation.

In this chapter, we look back through the nave, away from the altar, and head toward the cathedral's door, the threshold where sacred and secular meet. Here we examine one of the most extraordinary texts produced by any council in all of Christian history. It is the document that completes Vatican II's set of four constitutions: *Gaudium et Spes* ("Joy and

Hope"), the Pastoral Constitution on the Church in the Modern World, the final version of what during the council was known as *Schema 13*.

Joy and...Anguish

Gaudium et Spes picks up where the Dogmatic Constitution on the Church leaves off. It places the mystery of the Church in the context of a world defined by "the mystery that is man" (*GS* 10). Reminiscent of Vatican II's first publication, the "Message to Humanity," the Pastoral Constitution is the council's most daring statement. Critics find fault with what they call its naïve assessment of the "signs of the times" (*GS* 4). Many readers, popes included, have praised its affirmation of hope in an age of anxiety. John Paul II, who participated in the drafting of the constitution, made *Gaudium et Spes* a pillar of his defense of human dignity. For him, the document was the council's way of saying that "the mystery of redemption should be seen in light of the great renewal of man and of all that is human" (*Crossing the Threshold of Hope*, 48).

The constitution's prologue sets the tone for the document's overall message. It is one of the most frequently quoted passages from Vatican II:

> *The joy and hope, the grief and anguish of the men of our time, especially of those who are poor or afflicted in any way, are the joy and hope, the grief and anguish of the followers of Christ as well. Nothing that is genuinely human fails to find an echo in their hearts. For theirs is a community composed of men, of men who, united in Christ and guided by the holy Spirit, press onwards towards the kingdom of the Father and are bearers of a message of salvation intended for all men. That is why Christians cherish a feeling of deep solidarity with the human race and its history* (GS 1).

The Plan of the Constitution

Gaudium et Spes is Vatican II's longest document. It is also the longest document produced by any ecumenical council. Divided into two major parts, it offers a unique appraisal of the contemporary human experience and an equally unique response to its special problems.

The chapters of Part One speak to four specific topics: (1) the dignity of the human person, (2) the human community, (3) the role of humanity in the universe, and (4) the role of the Church in the modern world. The chapters of Part Two cover (1) marriage and family life, (2) the development of cultures, (3) economic justice and the value of work and leisure, (4) politics and public life, and (5) peace and international cooperation.

The constitution views the contemporary human situation through the lens of Christian faith. It is not a sociological study of the solitary individual or the secular crowd but a theological meditation on the human person, especially as shaped by the distinctive qualities of modern life, positive and negative. The details are taken from the changing data of modern society, but the meaning comes from revelation. Jesus Christ—"the same yesterday, and today, and forever" (*GS* 10; see Hebrews 13:8)—is the hinge upon which the whole constitution turns.

Christ at the Center

Despite Vatican II's pastoral orientation, the council fathers never shied from the obligation to teach Christian doctrine. In his opening speech, Pope John actually encouraged the bishops to take a bold stand for truth. "The greatest concern of the Ecumenical Council," he said, "is this: that the sacred deposit of Christian doctrine should be guarded and taught more efficaciously" (Abbott 713).

We might expect only the council's "dogmatic" constitutions to deal seriously with questions of doctrine. A close reading of the whole collection, however, shows us that even the more practical documents address significant doctrinal matters. All four of the constitutions contribute especially to the doctrine at the core of Christian faith: Christology (the doctrine of the person and work of Christ). As Pope

Benedict has said, "The foremost intention of the council was to reveal [the] need for Christ in the depth of the human heart" (*Theological Highlights of Vatican II*, 244).

The Constitution on the Sacred Liturgy, for example, speaks eloquently of the living presence of Christ in the Church:

> *Christ is always present in his Church, especially in her liturgical celebrations. He is present in the Sacrifice of the Mass not only in the person of his minister...but especially in the eucharistic species. By his power he is present in the sacraments so that when anybody baptizes it is really Christ himself who baptizes. He is present in his word since it is he himself who speaks when the holy scriptures are read in the Church. Lastly, he is present when the Church prays and sings...(SC 7).*

Dei Verbum devotes many pages to Christ's decisive role in revelation. One of its most beautiful Christological statements comes from the first chapter:

> *After God had spoken many times and in various ways through the prophets, "in these last days he has spoken to us by a Son" (Hebrews 1:1-2). For he sent his Son, the eternal Word who enlightens all men, to dwell among men and to tell them about the inner life of God. Hence, Jesus Christ, sent as "a man among men," "speaks the words of God" (John 3:34), and accomplishes the saving work which the Father gave him to do (see John 5:36, 17:4). As a result, he himself—to see whom is to see the Father (see John 14:9)—completed and perfected Revelation and confirmed it with divine guarantees. He did this by the total fact of his presence and self-manifestation—by words and works, signs and miracles, but above all by his death and glorious resurrection from the dead, and finally by sending the Spirit of truth. He revealed that God was with us...(DV 4).*

For its part, *Lumen Gentium* also keeps a close focus on Christ the "light of humanity" (*LG* 1). This passage, on the intimate relationship between Christ and his Church, is a miniature catechism:

> *The head of this body is Christ. He is the image of the invisible God and in him all things came into being. He is before all creatures and in him all things hold together. He is the head of the body which is the Church. He is the beginning, the firstborn from the dead, that in all things he might hold the primacy (see Colossians 1:15-18). By the greatness of his power he rules heaven and earth, and with his all-surpassing perfection and activity he fills the whole body with the riches of his glory...(LG 7).*

Christ in *Gaudium et Spes*

Christ is also at the center of *Gaudium et Spes*. The constitution is famous for its call for a "new humanism" (*GS* 55)—a generous appreciation for the value and even holiness of human life and creativity. The Church, however, can never endorse a secular or "earthbound" humanism (*GS* 56). The reference point for any authentic humanism is always Jesus—the meeting point for God and humankind (see 1 Timothy 2:5): "The key, the center and the purpose of the whole of man's history is to be found in its Lord and Master" (*GS* 10).

Two sections on Christ serve as anchors for the constitution's theology of Christian humanism. Section 22, "Christ the New Man," offers a highly engaging portrait of the union of divine and human in Jesus. The incarnate *Logos* shows us the true meaning of human life:

In reality it is only in the mystery of the Word made flesh that the mystery of man truly becomes clear. For Adam, the first man, was a type of him who was to come, Christ the Lord, Christ the new Adam…[Christ] fully reveals man to himself and brings to light his most high calling….He who is the "image of the invisible God" (Colossians 1:15), is himself the perfect man who has restored in the children of Adam that likeness to God which had been disfigured ever since the first sin. Human nature, by the very fact that it was assumed, not absorbed, in him, has been raised in us also to a dignity beyond compare. For, by his Incarnation, he, the son of God, has in a certain way united himself with each man. He worked with human hands, he thought with a human mind. He acted with a human will, and with a human heart he loved.

Section 45 is called "Christ: Alpha and Omega." It reminds us that Christ—and we ourselves—can be properly understood only in cosmic perspective: "The Word of God, through whom all things were made, was made flesh, so that as a perfect man he could save all men and sum up all things in himself. The Lord is the goal of human history, the focal point of the desires of history and civilization, the center of mankind, the joy of all hearts, and the fulfillment of all aspirations."

Mystery and…Misery

Set against the horizon of Christ, the constitution's portrait of humanity is stunning and sobering. The document describes human beings as marvelously complex. We are made in the image of God, composed of body and soul, and endowed with rights, reason, freedom, and conscience—the echo of God's voice in the human heart (*GS* 16). We are not lone individuals in an indifferent universe, nor is the human race "just a speck of nature" (*GS* 14). We share in "the light of the divine mind" and surpass the "world of mere things" (*GS* 15). We are designed for life in community with each other and destined for eternal union with God.

At the same time, we are sinners in a fallen world. Inner conflict seems almost part of our natural makeup. Any objective analysis of the human condition must agree with the verdict of revelation: the life of the human is "a struggle, and a dramatic one, between good and evil, between light and darkness." Even at our best moments, we do the right things for the wrong reasons. We recognize ourselves in what the Bible says about the tragic tension between humanity's "high calling" and the "deep misery" that so often haunts earthly experience (*GS* 13).

Gaudium et Spes goes on to say that humans are particularly impressive and vulnerable in the modern situation. Astonishing advancements in medicine, education, transportation, and communication are accompanied by moral drift and "spiritual uneasiness" (*GS* 5). We are authors and victims of a world "at once powerful and weak, capable of doing what is noble and what is base, disposed to freedom and slavery, progress and decline, brotherhood and hatred" (*GS* 9).

What especially catches our eye today is the constitution's prophetic word on faith and science. Breakthroughs in knowledge and skill are signs of human greatness, but they also bring grave risks. *Gaudium et Spes* cautions against dangerous notions of the autonomy or moral neutrality of scientific research:

> *If by the term "the autonomy of earthly affairs" is meant that material being does not depend on God and that man can use it as if it had no relation to its creator, then the falsity of such a claim will be obvious to anyone who believes in God. Without a creator there can be no creature….Besides, once God is forgotten, the creature is lost sight of as well* (GS 36).

The Age of Atheism

This reference to forgetting God reminds us of Vatican II's unusual place in history. We sometimes refer to the Second Vatican Council as the Church's response to the scientific and industrial revolutions. The council was also, in a sense, the Church's response to the Russian Revolution. Vatican II was very much a Cold War council. The Cuban missile crisis occurred during its first session. The Soviet Union's official atheism was a fact of contemporary life.

Vatican II was the first council to reckon seriously with modern atheism. Never before had the denial or rejection of God been so widespread and seemingly so normal. Other councils have contended with competing faiths. Vatican II was the first to face the phenomenon of no faith.

The analysis of atheism in *Gaudium et Spes* is the Church's first systematic study of "one of the most serious problems of our time." The document outlines the types of atheism in modern culture and seeks to identify their causes. Christians must take their fair share of responsibility for the rise of unbelief: "To the extent that they are careless about their instruction in the faith, or present its teachings falsely, or even fail in their religious, moral, or social life, they must be said to conceal rather than to reveal the true nature of God and of religion" (*GS* 19).

The constitution encourages Catholics to answer atheism with credible presentations of Christian doctrine and the "witness of a living and mature faith" (*GS* 21). It also calls for dialogue with atheists. During Vatican II, Paul VI established a totally unprecedented Church agency to pursue this goal: the Secretariat for Non-Believers (later integrated into the Pontifical Council for Culture). Since the council, engagement with atheism has become an increasingly important feature of Catholic intellectual life.

Other Modern Challenges

The second part of *Gaudium et Spes* moves us from the realm of ideas to some of the thorniest problems in modern experience: sexuality, economics, race, politics, and international relations, to name just a few. All of these issues still dominate Catholic social teaching. Many of them set the stage for the great social encyclicals of the Vatican II popes—from Paul VI's *Populorum Progressio* (1967) to Benedict XVI's *Caritas in Veritate* (2009).

Here we should remember that Vatican II took place on the eve of a massive cultural revolution. The council fathers were keenly aware of the accelerating pace of history, but they did not anticipate the enormous changes in moral standards that would soon sweep the globe. *Gaudium et Spes* mentions abortion twice (GS27, 51), says nothing about homosexuality, and refers only briefly to the status of women (GS9, 29, 60, 67). It does, however, speak forcefully about the importance of the family, the rights of labor, and the need to work for the common good. What it says about marriage is extremely relevant in our day: "Authentic married love will be held in high esteem, and healthy public opinion will be quick to recognize it, if Christian spouses give outstanding witness to faithfulness and harmony in their love..." (GS 49).

The bishops were particularly concerned about war—especially modern war, distinguished, as they said, by "barbarities far surpassing those of former ages" (GS 79). Most had lived through two world wars. Many were still helping their people recover from the most recent global conflict, repairing or rebuilding bombed-out churches and mourning the thousands of priests, religious, and lay people who perished during the war. All of the council fathers were deeply troubled by the post-war arms race and the threat of nuclear holocaust.

Inspired by John XXIII's encyclical *Pacem in Terris* (1963), the bishops believed the time had come for a "completely fresh reappraisal of war" and even the banning of war itself. They singled out the practice of total war for special condemnation: "Every act of war directed to the indiscriminate destruction of whole cities or vast areas with their inhabitants is a crime against God and man" (GS 80). Today, these concerns, aggravated by terrorism and black-market traffic in weapons of mass destruction, are vital parts of the Church's teaching on the "danger of modern warfare" (*CCC* 2314).

The Pastoral Constitution on the Church in the Modern World, however, does not end on a note of despair: "The Church...has not lost hope" (*GS* 82). The first word published by Vatican II was a declaration of God's love for the world: "We believe that the Father so loved the world that He gave His own Son to save it" (Abbott 4). The council's last constitution concludes with that same sense of supernatural confidence. In fact, looking out on the world from the door of the cathedral, all we see is Christ: "It is the Father's will that we should recognize Christ our brother in the persons of all men and love them with an effective love, in word and in deed, thus bearing witness to the truth; and it is his will that we should share with others the mystery of his heavenly love. In this way men all over the world will awaken to a lively hope..." (*GS* 93).

CHAPTER SEVEN

The Church in Mission and Dialogue

During its closing ceremonies, Pope Paul VI commented on the exceptional character of the Second Vatican Council. The most Church-centered council in history had also turned out to be the most human-centered. "The Church in Council has been concerned," the Holy Father observed, "not only with herself and her relationship with God, but also with man—man as he really is today." After many months of reflection and deliberation, the true "keynote" of the historic event had finally been revealed: "All this rich teaching is channeled in one direction, the service of men....The Church has, so to speak, declared herself the servant of humanity" (Galli 289, 295).

Appropriately, then, we conclude our tour of Vatican II's cathedral of ideas in the piazza or public square outside the cathedral itself. The cathedral's majestic façade is now behind us, and all before us is God's good but fallen creation—the "earthly city" so tied up with the complex and storied human experience (GS 40). In the shadow of the structure made holy by the body and blood of Christ, we take the presence of the living Christ into this city, the world "so loved" by God (John 3:16).

The documents discussed in this final chapter reflect Vatican II's unmistakable orientation toward service. They extend the vision of *Gaudium et Spes* to every aspect of the Church's encounter with modern human experience and chart unexpected paths for the Church's pilgrimage toward the "heavenly city" (GS 57). These remarkable texts—four decrees and three declarations—highlight the growing edges of Vatican II's vision of a renewed Church on mission. In them we hear the mature voice of the council at its most earnest and urgent.

Education

Three of these documents contribute specifically to the fulfillment of our Lord's Great Commission: "Go therefore and make disciples of all nations, baptizing them in the name of the Father and of the Son and of the Holy Spirit, and teaching them to obey everything that I have commanded you" (Matthew 28:19-20). The Declaration on Christian Education emphasizes the significance of the teaching task, remembering that before all else Jesus himself was a teacher (see John 1:38). The document's Latin title drives its main point home all by itself: *Gravissimum Educationis*, the "paramount importance of education" (*GE* Preface). Contrary to those who would limit religion to pious feelings or blind belief, the declaration celebrates the life of the mind. The "intellectual apostolate" (*GE* 11) is not a luxury or sideline but a core element of the Catholic way of life.

The text affirms two fundamental rights: the human right to education, including the "sacred right" of all people to moral education (*GE* 1), and the Christian right to Christian education. It defends the family's divinely determined role in culture and the rights of parents in education. It also honors those who dedicate their lives to the teaching profession.

One of the most conspicuous features of the document is its countercultural viewpoint. It goes against the grain of modern trends that would redefine education as career preparation: "True education is directed towards the formation of the human person in view of his final end and the good of that society to which he belongs..." (*GE* 1). Education from a Catholic perspective must always be truly "catholic"—broad-ranging, holistic, taking into account every dimension of human experience, especially the transcendent. Knowledge "illumined by faith" (*GE* 8) and enhanced by a sense of values is the timeless Catholic ideal.

Missionary Activity

Along with education comes evangelization (from the Greek *evangelion*, "good news")—the spread of the Gospel. Again, the document's title says it all: *Ad Gentes*, "to the nations" (*AG* 1). Vatican II's Decree on the Church's Missionary Activity matches the council's growing global consciousness with a full-scale theology of global evangelization. Its message is the centrality of the missionary enterprise: "The Church on earth is by its very nature missionary" (*AG* 2).

Much has been said over the years about the so-called progressive spirit of Vatican II. Pope Benedict XVI, who participated in the writing of *Ad Gentes*, locates the truly progressive dimension of the council in its missionary outlook (*The Ratzinger Report*, 13). By the 1960s, many mainline Protestant denominations were diluting or even denying the Great Commission. Some had already reduced the missionary to a social worker. At Vatican II, the Catholic Church reaffirmed a dynamic and multifaceted understanding of the missionary mandate:

*The mission of the Church is carried out by means of that activity through which, in obedience to Christ's command and moved by the grace and love of the Holy Spirit, the Church makes itself fully present to all men and peoples in order to lead them to the faith, freedom and peace of Christ by the example of its life and teaching, by the sacraments and other means of grace. Its aim is to open up for all men a free and sure path to full participation in the mystery of Christ (*AG 5).*

The decree on missions is one of Vatican II's most theologically compelling documents. It served as the inspiration for John Paul II's epic encyclical *Redemptoris Missio* (1990) and became the model for the section on missions in the *Catechism of the Catholic Church* (849–856). In it we find the ideas that make the Catholic approach to missions so distinctive: (1) the absolute uniqueness of Jesus Christ, the world's only Savior; (2) the necessity of faith and the sacraments of his Church for salvation; (3) the mysterious presence of elements of "truth and grace" and "seeds of the Word" in non-Christian traditions; and (4) the need to adapt the Christian message to the unique gifts and genius of every culture (*AG* 9, 11; see *LG* 14, 16).

The decree speaks eloquently of the diversity of cultures and the wideness of God's mercy: "God can lead those who, through no fault of their own, are ignorant of the Gospel to that faith without which it is impossible to please him" (*AG* 7). Never, though, does it border on relativism. In an age marked by a strange mixture of indifference and intolerance, we would do well to hear again the decree's universal call to a missionary spirituality:

> *The principal duty of both men and women is to bear witness to Christ...So all the children of the Church should have a lively consciousness of their own responsibility for the world, they should foster within themselves a truly Catholic spirit, they should spend themselves in the work of the Gospel.... [L]et everyone be aware that the primary and most important contribution he can make to the spread of the faith is to lead a profound Christian life. Their fervor in the service of God and their love for others will be like a new spiritual breeze throughout the whole Church...*(AG 21, 36).

Mass Communication

Vatican II enhanced its reflections on educational and evangelistic outreach with practical considerations of method and morality. We know *what* the Christian message is, *who* should receive it, and *why* they need to hear it. But *how* shall the Church get its message to the world? The Decree on the Instruments of Social Communication encourages Catholics to master the science and technique of film, radio, television, and other forms of mass communication in order "to propagate and defend the truth and to secure the permeation of society by Christian values" (*IM* 17).

The document concentrates on the right of every citizen to be informed, the rights of art itself, and also the responsibility of Catholics to think critically and creatively about the proper uses of the mass media. From the printing press to television (and now, we would say, the Internet and other digital media), every stage in the evolution of popular communication has offered the Church a new opportunity to be "salt and light" in the world (*IM* 24). The ongoing challenge is to balance technical efficiency with faithfulness to the "objective moral order" (*IM* 6).

The Apostolate of Dialogue

Vatican II reenergized Catholic education and evangelization, but there was nothing particularly new about these subjects for the council fathers. Both had been forms of Catholic outreach since the beginning of the Church. Even mass communication was not new. The Church had been quick to exploit the potential of Gutenberg's movable type in the 1400s, and Benedict XI, the first pope to address a radio audience, embraced the information technology of his day, some thirty years before the Second Vatican Council.

The new form of outreach at Vatican II was dialogue. The bishops' endorsement of respectful, two-way interaction between the Church and the world transposed Catholic solidarity with the human community into a new key. Never before had an ecumenical council obliged Catholics, especially Catholic leaders, to teach, preach, and defend the faith—and, at the same time, to "play their part in dialogue with the world and with men of all shades of opinion" (*GS* 43).

Pope John XXIII opened the door to dialogue when he emphasized the need to restore the "seamless garment of the Church" in his pre-council encyclicals (*Ad Petri Cathedram*, 81). Today we see his creation of the Secretariat for Promoting Christian Unity and his decision to address *Pacem in Terris* to "all men of good will" as milestones on the way to a theology of dialogue.

Paul VI, however, must be acknowledged as the first true pope of dialogue. He elevated dialogue to the level of an official goal for Vatican II and made it a defining theme of his pontificate. His encyclical *Ecclesiam Suam* (1964) was the first papal letter dedicated to dialogue in the history of the Church. Its image of four concentric circles of dialogue—within the Catholic community itself, with non-Catholic Christians, with non-Christian people of faith, and with the world at large—established dialogue as a permanent fixture of magisterial thought. His new Vatican departments, the Secretariat for Non-Christians (1964) and the Secretariat for Non-Believers (1965), officially transformed the Catholic Church into a Church of dialogue. "Our dialogue," Paul said, "should be as universal as we can make it" (*Ecclesiam Suam*, 76).

Ecumenical Dialogue

Vatican II's commitment to dialogue developed along two specific tracks: (1) dialogue with fellow Christians (ecumenical dialogue) and (2) dialogue with non-Christian believers (interfaith or interreligious dialogue). We have already seen how the word "ecumenical" (from the Greek for "whole world") had long been used to describe the special authority of bishops' councils in the formation of Christian doctrine. By Vatican II, a new layer of meaning had been added to the term. Church leaders were now using "ecumenical"—along with "ecumenism"—to refer to the quest for unity among Christian groups. Christ's high priestly prayer became the watchword of the modern ecumenical movement: "that they may all be one" (John 17:21).

The council's Decree on Eastern Catholic Churches reminds us that real dialogue begins inside the Church. The document honors the Catholics of the Middle East and Eastern Europe (Eastern-rite Catholics) and strikes the supremely Catholic note of diversity-in-unity. It expresses admiration for the special liturgies, unique organizations, rich cultures, and "ancestral traditions" that these historic communities bring to Catholic experience (*OE* 5). The document also looks forward to the time when Catholics and Christians in the Orthodox churches will enjoy the undivided fellowship known to Christ's earliest disciples: "All Christians, Eastern and Western, are strongly urged to pray to God daily with fervor and constancy in order that, by the help of God's most holy Mother, all may be one" (*OE* 30).

The Decree on Ecumenism, *Unitatis Redintegratio*, inaugurated a new age of dialogue among Christians of all kinds. Few Vatican documents have had a greater impact on Christian belief and behavior. Thirty years after its release, in the first papal encyclical ever written on the subject, Pope John Paul II recognized ecumenism as an "organic part" of the Church's life and work (*Ut Unum Sint*, 20).

The decree takes us back to the original aims of the council: "The restoration of unity among all Christians is one of the principal concerns of the Second Vatican Council" (*UR* 1; see *SC* 1). It identifies "elements and endowments" of authentic Christianity outside the boundaries of the Catholic Church, calls for sincere dialogue with the "separated brethren" of the Orthodox and Protestant traditions, and encourages Catholics to take their share of the blame for the divisions that have plagued world Christianity. At the same time, it warns against compromising fundamental principles in the interest of Christian reunion. The unity of Christ's one and only Church, the decree makes clear, "subsists in the Catholic Church" (*UR* 3–4; see *LG* 8).

Above all, the decree highlights the uniquely spiritual dimension of the new ecumenical vocation:

> *There can be no ecumenism worthy of the name without interior conversion….The faithful should remember that they promote union among Christians better, that indeed they live it better, when they try to live holier lives according to the Gospel. For the closer their union with the Father, the Word, and the Spirit, the more deeply and easily will they be able to grow in mutual brotherly love. This change of heart and holiness of life, along with public and private prayer for the unity of Christians, should be regarded as the soul of the whole ecumenical movement...(UR 7–8).*

Interfaith Dialogue

Both Christian ecumenism and the "wider ecumenism" of interfaith outreach are based on respect for the integrity of each individual's religious experience. The council's Declaration on Religious Freedom, the Church's first official defense of universal religious liberty, presents a thoroughly Catholic argument for the rights of conscience. Its case turns on (1) God's natural and supernatural revelation of the moral law, (2) the dignity and essential freedom of the human conscience, and (3) the obligation of every person to seek the truth. Civil governments do not possess the authority to interfere with the "free exercise of religion" (*DH* 3)—either of individuals or of groups, including the family. Freely pursuing the truth in the context of social life is not an optional aspect of human experience but the "highest of man's rights and duties" (*DH* 15).

The Declaration on the Relationship of the Church to Non-Christian Religions builds on this fundamental appreciation for the rights of conscience. It is the council's shortest document and one of its most provocative—though sadly unknown to many Catholics. John Paul II, whose passion for interfaith affairs was surpassed only by his enthusiasm for ecumenism, called the text "the Magna Carta of interreligious dialogue for our times" (*Ecclesia in Asia*, 31).

Nostra Aetate affirms the uniqueness of God's revelation in Jesus Christ and the knowledge of God beyond institutional Christianity. Its inclusive view of non-Christian traditions has become one of the most distinctive features of contemporary Catholic thought (see *CCC* 836-848):

The Catholic Church rejects nothing of what is true and holy in these religions. She has a high regard for the manner of life and conduct, the precepts and doctrines which, although differing in many ways from her own teaching, nevertheless often reflect a ray of that truth which enlightens all men. Yet she proclaims and is in duty bound to proclaim without fail, Christ who is the way, the truth and the life (John 14:6). In him, in whom God reconciled all things to himself (2 Corinthians 5:18–19), men find the fullness of their religious life (NA 2).

The declaration commends the beauty and wisdom of the Hindu, Buddhist, and Muslim traditions—and even the aspirations of religions that vaguely seek a "hidden power" in or behind nature. Written by leaders who had witnessed the horrors of the Holocaust, however, it devotes most of its attention to the "common spiritual heritage" shared by Jews and Christians. Its condemnation of anti-Semitism dramatically revolutionized Jewish-Christian relations:

Indeed, the Church reproves every form of persecution against whomsoever it may be directed....There is no basis therefore, either in theory or in practice, for any discrimination between individual and individual, or between people and people arising either from human dignity or from the rights which flow from it. Therefore, the Church reproves, as foreign to the mind of Christ, any discrimination against people or any harassment of them on the basis of their race, color, condition in life or religion (NA 4–5).

The Legacy of Dialogue

Since the appearance of *Nostra Aetate* in 1965, we have lived through an almost unbelievable transformation in Catholic relations with other believers. Two unprecedented events from the pontificate of John Paul II demonstrate just how much ground has been covered since the council. At the first World Day of Prayer for Peace in Assisi (1986), rabbi, guru, swami, minister, imam, and shaman came together at the request of the pope for an unforgettable moment of shared contemplation. On the First Sunday of Lent in the Jubilee Year of 2000, the pope invited all Catholics to pray for forgiveness for sins against the Jewish people and members of other religions. Few events could more forcefully communicate Vatican II's call for an ecumenical "change of heart" (*UR* 8). Nothing could portray so perfectly John Paul's verdict on the council as a whole: "*The Second Vatican Council was a great gift to the Church*, to all those who took part in it, to the entire human family, and to each of us individually" (*Crossing the Threshold of Hope*, 157).

,

Conclusion

In Europe's great age of faith, the cathedral raised the eye of peasant and prince to a reality far transcending their world of village, field, and feudal loyalty. A monument to human ingenuity and the glory of God, it was indeed a "bible of stone"—a brilliant translation of the Gospel into the alphabet of architecture. From its giant portals to its radiant altar, the cathedral set before the medieval mind the horizon of God's "mystery hidden for ages and generations but now made manifest to his saints" (Colossians 1:26, RSV).

The documents of the Second Vatican Council witness to that same mystery. Products of remarkable craft and genius in their own right, they stand as a temple of truth on the landscape of the secular city—a cathedral of ideas, measured not in cubic feet and tons but in words, pages, gigabytes, and moral weight. Simply as literature, the documents deserve to be ranked among the most significant books of the modern age.

Documents, however, cannot read themselves. A stone cathedral is little more than a heap of masonry to the untrained eye. In order to penetrate to its inner meaning, we have to interpret it according to the rules of its special grammar—walk around it, sit before it, watch its transformation from dawn to dusk, like master Monet behind his famous easel.

At the beginning of this century, John Paul II called for a new season of engagement with the documents of his beloved Vatican II. "*It is time for deep reflection on the council's teaching,*" he declared (*Address to the Conference Studying the Implementation of Vatican II*, 9). The tourist or pilgrim departs a great cathedral rejuvenated, inspired, and perhaps overwhelmed. What awaits the sincere reader of the Vatican II texts is a life-changing encounter with the living Church and the Church's living Lord.

Works Cited

Abbott, Walter M., ed. *The Documents of Vatican II*. New York: America Press, 1966.

Balthasar, Hans Urs von. *The Glory of the Lord*. Trans. Oliver Davies, *et al.* 7 vols. San Francisco: Ignatius Press, 1982-1991.

Catechism of the Catholic Church. 2nd ed. Washington, DC: United States Catholic Conference, 1997. Cited as *CCC*.

Center for Applied Research in the Apostolate. http://cara.georgetown.edu.

The Encyclicals and Other Messages of John XXIII. Ed. Staff of *The Pope Speaks* Magazine. Washington, DC: TPS Press, 1964. Cited as *Encyclicals*.

Flannery, Austin, ed. *Vatican Council II: The Conciliar and Post Conciliar Documents*. Rev. ed. Northport, NY: Costello, 1996.

Galli, Mario von and Bernhard Moosbrugger. *The Council and the Future*. New York: McGraw-Hill, 1966.

Howell, Kenneth J., trans. *Ignatius of Antioch and Polycarp of Smyrna*. Zanesville, OH: CHResources, 2009.

Hugo, Victor. *Notre-Dame of Paris*. Trans. John Sturrock. New York: Penguin Books, 2004.

John Paul II. *Crossing the Threshold of Hope*. Ed. Vittorio Messori. Trans. Jenny McPhee and Martha McPhee. New York: Alfred A. Knopf, 1994.

Joyce, James. *Finnegans Wake*. New York: Penguin Books, 1999.

Küng, Hans, Yves Congar, and Daniel O'Hanlon, eds. *Council Speeches of Vatican II*. Glen Rock, NJ: Paulist Press, 1964. Cited as *Council Speeches*.

Maritain, Jacques. *On the Church of Christ*. Trans. Joseph W. Evans. Notre Dame: University of Notre Dame Press, 1973.

Paul VI. *Address to a General Audience*. November 26, 1969. www.ewtn.com/library/papaldoc/p6691126.htm.

Ratzinger, Joseph. *Theological Highlights of Vatican II*. Trans. Werner Barzel, Gerard Thormann, Henry Traub. New York: Paulist Press, 2009.

Ratzinger, Joseph, and Vittorio Messori. *The Ratzinger Report*. Trans. Salvator Attanasio and Graham Harrison. San Francisco: Ignatius Press, 1985.

Scharper, Philip J. *Meet the American Catholic*. Nashville, TN: Broadman Press, 1969.

Tanner, Norman P., ed. *Decrees of the Ecumenical Councils*. 2 vols. London and Washington, DC: Sheed and Ward, Georgetown University Press, 1990.

Suggestions for Further Reading

Alberigo, Giuseppe. *A Brief History of Vatican II*. Trans. Matthew Sherry. Maryknoll, NY: Orbis Books, 2006.

Bellitto, Christopher M., ed. *Rediscovering Vatican II*. 8 vols. New York: Paulist Press, 2005-2009.

Hahnenberg, Edward P. *A Concise Guide to the Documents of Vatican II*. Cincinnati, OH: St. Anthony Messenger Press, 2007.

Huebsch, Bill. *Vatican II in Plain English*. 3 vols. Notre Dame, IN: Ave Maria Press, 1997.

Huff, Peter A. *Vatican II: Its Impact on You*. Liguori, MO: Liguori Publications, 2011.

Lamb, Matthew, and Matthew Levering. *Vatican II: Renewal Within Tradition*. New York: Oxford University Press, 2009.

O'Malley, John W. *What Happened at Vatican II*. Cambridge, MA: Harvard University Press, 2008.

Schreck, Alan. *Vatican II: The Crisis and the Promise*. Cincinnati, OH: Servant Publications, 2005.

Sullivan, Maureen. *101 Questions and Answers on Vatican II*. New York: Paulist Press, 2002.

Vorgrimler, Herbert, ed. *Commentary on the Documents of Vatican II*. Trans. L. Adolphus, K. Smyth, and R. Strachan. 5 vols. New York: Herder and Herder, 1967-1969.

Whitehead, Kenneth D. *The Renewed Church: The Second Vatican Council's Enduring Teaching about the Church*. Ave Maria, FL: Sapientia Press, 2009.

Wojtyła, Karol. *Sources of Renewal: The Implementation of the Second Vatican Council*. Trans. P. S. Falla. San Francisco: Harper and Row, 1979.